From Michael de Freitas to Michael X

From Michael de Freitas to

Michael X

by Michael Abdul Malik

ANDRE DEUTSCH

FIRST PUBLISHED 1968 BY
ANDRE DEUTSCH LIMITED
105 GREAT RUSSELL STREET
COPYRIGHT © 1968 BY MICHAEL ABDUL MALIK
ALL RIGHTS RESERVED
PRINTED IN GREAT BRITAIN BY
CLARKE DOBLE & BRENDON LTD
PLYMOUTH

SBN 233 96019 8

Author's note

People the world over have always assumed that the English language of the black and the English language of the white is one and the same. This is a false assumption. There is a difference of both thought and expression which makes communication difficult. At one extreme some words used by whites will be found highly insulting by black people and doubtless some words used by blacks are offensive to white ears. This was the problem which was foremost in my mind when I first thought of producing this document.

I tried many ways to break the language barrier—using tapes, talking to various people, experimenting with interpreters—all to no avail. Then, through my agent, I was introduced to a straight-looking English cat, a writer I shall call John X. When I first saw him I doubted that he would ever understand anything I said and most certainly anything that I felt. I am happy to say I was completely mistaken. We achieved the small miracle of crashing the barrier together.

Over a period of two years, I spent many days with John, eating and drinking with him, going from place to place, talking. He visited the ghetto areas, chatted with my now deceased mother, observed me talking with my own people, joined in our social gatherings, made himself quietly acceptable—no easy thing for a white man inside a completely black scene. All this time he was writing down what I had done throughout the years, getting my personality on paper, recapturing feelings I had experienced at various times of my life, selecting, constructing, complementing me.

I give thanks to John for enabling this document to be compiled, for breaking the barriers of language and colour. It has not been easy for me to be honest about certain areas where I lay myself open to be hurt. But in this book we have recorded the truth as I see it.

MICHAEL ABDUL MALIK

9th August 1967

1

White is pretty; black is ugly. That's what my black mother used to tell me when I was a little boy in Trinidad. It was her way of saying white people were superior and that we should pattern ourselves on them. It expressed a feeling that too many black people have had for too long. They don't need to feel that way any more.

My mother was born in Barbados, a descendant of slaves. Her parents were Barbadians and she grew up in that peculiarly Barbadian atmosphere where all the blacks are trying desperately to be English. They even call the island 'Little England' and to my mother—who was one of the blackest people I know—the best people in the world were white. That's certainly one of the reasons she lived with my father, a Portuguese merchant she met when she moved to Trinidad.

I was born in Trinidad and the first word I ever spoke was 'coo-coo'. 'Coo-coo' is a mixture of corn meal, water and sliced okra which is popular in the West Indies. Most babies say 'mama' or 'dada' before they say anything else, but I said 'coo-coo'— which I think is significant. I have a very big appetite. I used to eat and drink a lot and everything I've done, I've done a lot of. I like people, too. I can't have enough of them.

I don't remember my early childhood too well and I hardly knew my father since he lived with my mother only in the early years. My one clear recollection at that time is of him coming to see me in a maroon car when I was at kindergarten. I remember him saying goodbye. He was a nice-looking man and I liked him. But I didn't know him.

Most of my early memories are of growing up in my grandmother's house in Belmont, which was then on the outskirts of Port of Spain, the capital, but is now a suburb. It was one of a number of little wooden houses built on stilts and scattered over a hillside between the city and the mountains. To enter it you had to climb a flight of wooden steps from the surrounding muddy ground. It was pretty bare inside and there wasn't much of a view through the windows—just the corrugated roofs of other houses in one direction and, in the other, a muddy back yard with a coldwater shower in a corrugated iron cubicle, a cesspit toilet and a plum tree.

There were three rooms altogether and eight people lived in them. My grandmother, who had bought the house for 250 dollars (about £50 at that time), was the boss. She was a stocky woman with a very big head of grey hair. She was very, very strong which wasn't surprising considering the amount of heavy manual work she did. She was always working: cooking, scrubbing the house down, washing everybody's clothes. I remember she would do the laundry in a huge wooden barrel with the top sliced off. It was nowhere near a tap and she was constantly carrying buckets of water to and fro and often had to manhandle the full tub from place to place, which she did with ease.

We all called her 'maam'—even my grandfather. He was a little hunchbacked schoolteacher who simply came and went. He was nothing next to the old lady.

The money to feed us came from her son, Uncle Hilton, whom everyone called 'papa'. He worked as a shoemaker and made quite a reasonable living—which I understood later he improved on by gambling quite a bit. Papa was a very happy person, fit and full of life. He owned things like roller skates and a bicycle and sometimes he would put on the skates and have races with other men on the street. He was very fast and skilful and, if we children could get out, we would run to the bottom of the hill to watch him and cheer him on.

His wife, my Aunt Ivy, was another piece of the background. She was a slender person, meticulous in dress and very clean. She was simply there in the house, completely overshadowed by my grandmother, quietly doing the dusting and the other jobs that delicate women do.

The rest of the household was made up of children. Me and my three cousins, two boys and a girl.

My favourite cousin was the younger boy Samuel, who was just about my age. He was as tall as his brother, Ethelbert, who was three years older, and he grew to be a strong boy like me. In fact, everyone always said we were just like brothers, that we were equally naughty. We had a great friendship going—and we still have.

Ethelbert—Tibby, as he was known—was very quiet and reserved and meant nothing to me. As for the girl, who was a year older still—I don't even remember her name.

The adults had the two bedrooms in the house and we four children slept on makeshift beds of rags on the pinewood floor of the sitting room. Later, Aunt Ivy had a baby to add to the crowding.

It didn't mean anything to me that my mother wasn't there. She worked as a domestic servant in a hotel in the city and visited us every so often. In the meantime I was quite happy playing with Samuel, and my grandmother loved us all. She was always grabbing us with her strong arms and hugging us half to death.

Port of Spain was a very exciting place to me in those days and one of the biggest treats my mother could give me was to come to Belmont early on Sunday morning and take me to the market in the city.

We would start the two-mile walk from the house to the market with our great straw baskets. A trickle of people would join us from the shade of houses and palm trees, calling out greetings, heading down the hillside. By the time we reached the bottom of the hill the trickle had become a stream which grew and grew until a whole ragged army, sweating and joking and chattering away converged on the city.

The city to me was a whole new fascinating world. It was big red trams clanking along their tracks. It was narrow streets of open-fronted shops crammed with bright-coloured bales of cheap cotton, cast-iron cooking pots, straw hats, trinkets. It was big stores and banks and coconut carts where Indian vendors sliced the heads off green coconuts with pirate cutlasses for the thirsty crowds to drink. It was shopkeepers in their doorways chatting in Chinese. It was Indian ladies in their pale-coloured saris. It was groups of haggling Syrians and well-dressed Portuguese. It was a legion of Negroes sitting in barbers' shops, drinking in cafés,

munching bananas, brushing past as they went about their unknown business.

And finally it was the food market.

The food market was our destination. A great covered area
in the centre of the town, open on all sides so you could gaze
along the aisles between the rows of stalls piled high with fruit
and vegetables, fish and meat. I would wander along behind my
mother, listening to the large market ladies pushing their wares.
They always dressed beautifully, these ladies, in a flare of bright
clothes and headscarves, and they spoke with a different accent
from other ladies, mixing patois with English. I was always asking
my mother what the patois words meant and she would say I
must have nothing to do with them. English was our tongue, she
would say, and if the ladies spoke to her in patois she invariably
answered in English. I liked the market ladies because they were
always happy and throwing back their heads in laughter and
handing children free melon and oranges.

All through the market, on the fruit, on the wet fish, on the
bloodsoaked meat, a great mass of flies was constantly darting
and buzzing. When you ordered your beef, the butcher would
wave a cloth over the meat and the flies would rise in a huge
cloud so that he could cut off the slice you wanted.

Like everyone else on those noisy, crowded Sunday mornings,
we would fill our baskets to the full with good things and the final
buy would be a live chicken for Sunday lunch. Then the army of
shoppers would head back towards the outskirts, filling the trams
to overflowing, all weighed down with their baskets, making sure
that the chicken's head—a great status symbol—was sticking out
for all the neighbours to see.

Occasionally my mother would take me back into Port of
Spain in the afternoon for a tram ride around the Savannah. This
was a huge, flat grass area with football fields and cricket pitches
laid out inside. Around its perimeter the rich people lived in
big white houses with glass in the windows. I would have to dress
in my very best clothes for this trip. My mother would point out
the Governor's house, the Botanical Gardens and how clean and
nicely painted the houses of the white folks were.

'One day when you're grown up we're going to live around
here,' she would say.

As well as Sundays, my mother sometimes visited us in the
evenings and brought presents. She picked up lots of goodies for

us in the hotel where she worked, so her visits were always very welcome.

Once she brought me a tricycle, new and bright and red, which we rode around the inside of the house. We weren't allowed to play outside in case we got dirty. White children never got dirty, so this was part of trying to be white. My grandmother wasn't quite as white-oriented as my mother, but she was much indoctrinated with this English pattern of behaviour; even her accent was English.

Sometimes when my grandmother and the other adults were away from the house we would go outside and play and get dirty and then we would be beaten—the English cure for un-English behaviour.

When I was about four years old, my mother got married to a local taxi driver and I went to live with them in another wooden house not far from my grandmother's. It was a nicer house on flat land with a yard that was clean and dry rather than swampy, and it had a guava tree in place of the plum tree. I was the only child so I had all the guavas.

I remember my mother and her mother-in-law didn't speak to each other. The mother-in-law complained that her son had married a woman older than himself, a woman who had a child by another man—a white man at that. She never came to the house. She would send messages for her son by his young nephews, who would wait somewhere outside to intercept him.

My stepfather was a big, heavy man. I was slightly afraid of him because he was new and because he never tried to be my friend. He hardly ever said a word to me, hardly seemed to notice me.

The first time I really knew he was aware of me was one day when my father was mentioned and a vicious row somehow started. I didn't understand it at all, but there was a lot of shouting and my stepfather was yelling: 'All he left you is a big cunt and a red bastard!' Red is the name for a half caste in the West Indies. My mother was proud of my colour, but my stepfather made it sound like a term of abuse. I got terribly frightened and hid under the house for hours so that they came out looking for me as it got dark.

There were more rows about my colour and my mother would send me out to play when they started, threatening to hit me if I didn't go, and then I would hear them fighting inside the house.

Afterwards, sometimes, when we were alone, my mother would make her pet statement : 'You don't know what I have to put up with.'

For some reason, though, I never took her side. I simply felt it was their own business.

I began to go to school around five years old—a mixed private school which was very snobbish. My mother was determined I should have a good education. When I grew up I would get a good job, she said, because, unlike her, I had a good colour. We had my father to thank for that. Whenever she referred to him she used the same phrase to describe him : 'white and pretty'.

I enjoyed school very much. I was very bright—always first in my class—and could run very fast. This was a combination which seemed to ensure that I had plenty of friends. There were white and black pupils at the school but no open prejudice, as I remember. At the age of seven I had my first girl friend—a little white girl named Lena. She came from a Catholic school, most of which practised discrimination, and I think I liked her because she was white and 'superior'. From then on I always had girl friends from those schools.

Mr Alexis, my schoolmaster—he owned the school—was a nice, fatherly type of Trinidadian. He had lots of children, including a boy around my own age with whom I was friendly. This son died from an operation and after that Mr Alexis seemed to develop a special liking for me as if he identified me a little with the dead boy. He was always showing me off to visitors, having me recite something to show how good his pupils were. He wanted everything nice in the world to happen to me and eventually suggested putting me in another school where I could have a chance of entering the Government Exhibitions and winning a free scholarship to a secondary school at the age of twelve.

Around that time the war had started and taxi drivers were making more money from the American bases and the fact that there were many more visiting seamen. My stepfather's income was rising, so I was allowed to take the exams to the new school.

The first year I was there my mother decided we should both join the Catholic Church. Her husband was a Catholic, but I think she got the religious bug because her brother had turned to some kind of voodoo cult, called obeah. She told me later that she took me to all the churches in the island to see which one I liked best and I chose the Rosary Church, the second biggest in Trinidad, though I don't remember this. What I do remember is that many strange people started visiting us around this time because, as it turned out, my mother was indulging in a little obeah herself, on the side.

It was all rather mysterious to me. All I knew was that people would come and remain closeted with my mother for a while and that afterwards there would always be extra presents for me or, perhaps, a new white chicken in the house. I think people brought livestock at my mother's request in the belief it was for some sort of sacrifice. In no time we had our whole yard full of poultry and we didn't need to buy chickens in the market any more.

One day I resolved to find out what was happening and I stayed in the next room when I knew someone was coming and peeked through a crack in the wall.

All the blinds were closed in the other room and my mother was sitting at a table with a candle burning on it next to a glass of water. She looked quite different from usual with a big, white cloth tied around her head and flowing down over her shoulders.

Sitting on the other side of the table with her eyes wide was this Trinidadian lady who'd lived in America for many years and recently returned to the island.

'I have a skin disease,' I heard her whisper. 'I gotta wear these black gloves. I been everywhere to get a cure.'

'Take off your gloves and show me your hands,' my mother said slowly. 'I can help you if you believe in me. If you don't believe, then there's no point in going on.'

'They tell me about you and I believe,' the woman said.

She began to peel off her gloves and I was quite terrified by the whole procedure. Even my mother's voice sounded different, speaking with deliberation and great authority. I began to believe she had some strange power and I didn't want any part of it, but I couldn't pull myself away.

My mother looked at the hands which the woman had rested on the table. She nodded wisely and said: 'If you give me fifty dollars I can cure you.'

The woman opened her bag and handed over fifty dollars without a word.

'And now you give me one penny,' my mother said, with gravity.

The penny was passed over and my mother rose and took a tin

of skin ointment from a shelf. She sat down again and leaned forward, gazing across the table at her client.

'Take this ointment and dip the penny in it,' she said, 'and then you rub the penny over the backs of your hands and put it on the ledge over your door. You do that for nine days and on the ninth day you go to a crossroads and throw the penny away. You don't have a mark on you after you do that and anyone who picks up the penny gets your disease.'

All the while my mother was talking, the woman's eyes were very big and wide and she was nodding between every two words. My eyes were even wider and as the woman left I held my breath and crept into the back yard.

The woman never came back to complain on the tenth day so I suppose she must have been satisfied with the treatment. I know that I never dared to pick any money off the ground after that.

The Rosary Church, which we joined, had white boys as acolytes serving mass; the black boys served at funerals. My mother insisted I join the acolytes serving mass and the priest said I would have to learn mass in Latin. To give me practice, my mother would give the priest money to say mass : that I would be good in class, for a dead sister I didn't even know I had, for anything she could think of. In the end, I served mass every day for six years.

There were fourteen white boys at church and I made the fifteenth. They always told me I had joined the wrong group and that I should be with the funerals. They made me very nervous. Some were merely unpleasant, but others would try nasty practical jokes like tipping over my stool at the altar. Those boys used to do everything they could to show me I was different from them, which wasn't all that surprising since at church you often heard phrases like 'black as sin' and 'pure as white'.

Finally, one night at a special celebration, one of the white boys brought presents for us all : white sugar cake made from grated coconut. If you added molasses, it turned dark and was called 'tulum'. There were twelve of us that night and he brought eleven sugar cakes and one tulum. From that moment on I carried a new name—Tulum.

Looking back, I see my parents didn't know how to deal with the colour question and they messed me up.

All these years later and across an ocean the problem is just the same. My five-year-old daughter was playing ring-a-ring-o-roses at Rotherfield School, Islington and the white girl next to her wouldn't take her hand. She wouldn't hold the hand of a black child. My daughter's getting the same scene I had: white is pretty; black is ugly.

But I'm not sitting back and letting the scene perpetuate itself. I'm trying to redress the balance in my own way.

My daughter's fond of drawing and I teach her to draw. I watch her for a while and every so often I say: 'Put a little more black in here. Black's a very pretty colour.'

2

Trinidad should be a great place for a boy to grow up in, but for me it was all ruined by my mother's hang-up about colour. She didn't want me doing anything the black boys did; didn't want me associating with them. She wanted me to be a little white boy because she didn't make it to be a white lady. She had a long list of 'don'ts' for me, covering just about everything that was fun and if I really wanted to have a good time I had to do it behind her back, or just run off and take a beating when I got back.

One of the things I particularly liked was going into the hills with other black boys to pick fruit and collect tropical fish. The hills rose up to 1,200 feet and were covered with exotic vegetation. There were silk cotton trees, massive mango trees, saperdillars (a brown fruit like a small pear), soursop (something like a prickly pear), sugar apples—all growing wild everywhere so that you could pick them on the way up and come down laden. This was strictly illegal, of course, and sometimes we were chased by irate landowners who had little huts hidden amongst the trees and would seem to materialise from thin air.

Once I was high up a mango tree shaking the fruit down for my friends. It was a special sort of mango called a mango calabash, whose fruit has smooth flesh rather like an avocado pear. We loved them and I was shaking like mad when I suddenly looked down to find my friends had taken off in all directions leaving a large and furious gentleman waving a cutlass at me from the foot of the tree. He started shouting for me to come down, brandishing the weapon as if he wanted to cut me in pieces. I was terrified and wouldn't move and he took out a pipe and sat under the branches smoking, telling me: 'All right—I'll wait.' At this I began to cry and scream for help, begging him: 'Give me a chance, give me a chance.' But he just sat there like a big spider waiting to get me, knowing I had to move some time.

I was at my wits' end and I seemed to be perched up there a lifetime before my friends came creeping back to the rescue. I saw them flitting back through the trees, coming as near as they dared before they started pelting him with a barrage of stones. Little boys in Trinidad have a pretty good aim and they gave him such a hard time that he finally took off after one who came closer than the others so that I was able to scamper down and tear off down the hillside, grabbing a few fruit in a surge of bravado as I went.

We used to collect the tropical fish from the little mountain springs and pools. Some of the boys would have jars with them and you could catch dozens of fish simply by dropping the jar, or a net, into a pool and pulling it straight out again. If we'd been able to catch the birds we'd have done that, too, because they were out of this world. Splurges of colour would dart amongst the leaves and the singing would never let up. There'd be a glimpse of canary-like piquoplats, of yellow-breasted kiss-kiddees, named after the sound of their constant whistle, of black-birds, bluebirds. . . .

At night, some of the older boys would go shooting wild animals —little rodents like the manicoci and the agouti and maybe a porcupine—while the rest of us would stalk iguanas.

It was so marvellous in the hills, so cool and free and unlike the sticky, sweaty city, that I wouldn't want to leave and wouldn't get home until late night so that even though I hid the fruit under the house my mother would know where I'd been. She would give me a knife and order me to cut a branch from the guava tree. This was the whip she would use on me as my punishment for being 'too hardened' and 'refusing to listen', which meant playing with the wrong boys.

She got worse when we moved to a more affluent part of Bel-mont where there were paved streets in place of dirt tracks and the houses were concrete instead of wood. I suppose this was because we were within sight of the sort of white area which meant so much to her, and it was all the more clear how comparative a term like affluent could be.

Our part of Belmont backed onto a broad concrete gulley called the Dry River which served as a sewer, its central gutter running with water and refuse even in the dry season. This rift in the land formed a division between Belmont and a white area with the resplendent name of Queen's Park West. On the white side the houses were neat and beautifully painted, with splendid verandahs, well-tended rose gardens, drive-ins, lace curtains—the hall-marks of affluence. On the black side all the paint was blistered and peeling, nothing much would grow in the unkempt gardens, the curtains were cotton instead of lace and there were no drive-ins since there were no cars.

With her envious eyes constantly directed across the Dry River, my mother couldn't stand the idea of my playing with the black boys in the gulley. I used to have to wait until she went shopping and then I'd slip off and join them in the games that were all the rage.

One of the favourites was 'running jockey', in which we would hold boat races in the water of the sewer. Boys would spend hours fashioning boats from bits of old wood, covering them with candle wax and lining them up for a race behind a piece of crate. When the board was lifted, the boats would go racing and twisting away to a finishing mark and the winner would get a few pennies.

Marbles was popular, too. Every boy would place four marbles in a ring scratched in the dust in someone's back yard. Then each in turn would throw a target marble and knock as many out of the circle as he could. You won all those you knocked out. I was not terribly good at it, so quite often the black boys would come to my yard to pitch so that they could win a lot of marbles. If my mother came back and found them, she was furious. She would pick up a cutlass—everyone has them in Trinidad to cut sugar cane—and run it along the floor as a warning before she chased them out shouting: 'You're too black to come in here!' When they'd fled for their lives, she would turn on me and say: 'How many times I tell you—never look under your feet for company; look up!' 'Up' meant white children and if ever they came to play her attitude was completely different. She'd get a great entertaining scene going, being very nice to them, providing ice cream and coca cola.

I was never invited to the white boys' homes and gradually my mother alienated me from most of my black friends.

Another thing she ruined for me was the event of the year in Trinidad—the Carnival. Everyone has wild fun for the Carnival. It goes on for a couple of never-ending days in a great haze of drink, laughter, streamers, dancing, music, costumes, giant floats, flowers, wild behaviour all crazily churned up in a heat of un-reality. Port of Spain vibrates to primitive steel bands made of biscuit tins, dustbins, rum bottles with about three notes between them. It is filled with black men walking around with white faces and claiming to be white minstrels. It is overrun with black devils dressed in horns and long tails made of cotton reels; with black Mexicans in huge sombreros and guns on their hips; with little black boys beating kerosene drums and dressed in bathing trunks with their bodies daubed with tar. The make-believe Mexicans called themselves robbers and they would hold everybody up with their guns and force them to listen to their poetry—fan-tastic, lyrical poetry about Trinidad which has died away be-cause it was never written down. If two robbers met, there was a wild scene with each shouting poetry at the other until one of them was drowned out.

The little black boys with the tarred bodies had a great scene going for themselves, too. They would terrorise people for money. If you didn't deliver, they'd rub themselves against you and mess your clothes up. They were never short of loot.

Altogether, it was impossible to watch this all going on with-out wanting to join in. But that was something 'social people' (the social-climbing middle class) never did and so my mother wouldn't allow me to have anything to do with the vulgar steel bands and the lower-class dancing. That was for the hooligans. Instead of letting me partake, she would lead me to the sedate Grandstand in the centre of the Savannah where the white people and the well-dressed Negro element went to watch the activity from a dignified distance. It was the 'correct' thing to do—mixing with the better classes. My mother, in common with the other Grand-stand people, would have much more admiration for the white floats where they performed masques and Greek play scenes and where the music was of an elegant string orchestral kind in place of the back-to-Africa type music of the blacks and the crash of the steel bands.

This racial obsession of my mother's coloured everything that happened in my childhood. Other boys would spend hours and days playing soccer and cricket in the Dry River but she forbade me to do that sort of thing, ostensibly to stop me getting hurt, but in fact because it was the sort of thing the niggers did and she didn't want me being identified with them. She used to vent her hatred on any black boys who tried to beat me up while she was around. She would be amongst them like a tigress, slapping their ears, quite prepared to take on their fathers too, revealing the motivation for this maternal protectiveness as she screamed at them : 'You can't beat up a white man child like that !'

Sometimes when I'd committed some mortal sin like going up into the hills with the black boys, or playing marbles in their back yards, she'd hold her head and scream at the top of her voice : 'Oh God help me ! What am I going to do with this boy !' She would scream and yell so long and hard that the neighbours from all around would come to their doors and start up towards our house thinking something terrible was happening to her. People would be saying : 'That child will kill his mother. . . . That boy's going to end up on the hangman's rope.'

I would feel so bad and wicked then that my eyes would almost fall out of my head and my veins stand out and I would desperately wonder what I could do to change from being so evil and upsetting my mother like that. She would give me five dollars for the priest and I would confess and he would order me to say ten Hail Marys as a penance while he stood over me, his red Irish face glowing and his breath stinking of too much liquor.

Maybe all this had something to do with why I failed four times to get a scholarship so that finally my mother paid for me to go to an exclusive secondary school called St Mary's College.

The college was a rather strange Catholic institution which cost sixteen dollars a term—quite a bit of money for those days. One of its principal features was its scout troops : an exclusive one for white children and several others for the blacks. I didn't belong to any of them due to the expense, but I have no doubt my mother would have moved heaven and earth to get me into the white troop had the money been there. And she might have succeeded. Being half white always got me half a foot in the door and a chance of crashing the white barrier.

Once settled in the new school, I began to get good marks again. In my first term I was eleventh in a class of thirty-five

and came top in geometry and arithmetic. I also represented my
class in elocution contests, which I loved from the beginning.

The college had something like 1,600 pupils and everyone
would assemble in the main hall for the contests. The students
would all be very quiet, listening, and a visiting dignitary would
join the masters on the judges' panel. From the beginning I never
felt any shyness or embarrassment as I read from my favourite
book of the time : *The Children of the New Forest*. I came second
the very first time I competed.

I had no problem getting along with the other children, but
by tacit agreement both white and black tended to keep in their
own groupings—even when walking home.

After I'd been at the school two years I was requested to
leave. I'd been giving the teachers a hard time and they'd been
sending me to the Dean on an average of once a week. My
trouble was talking in class. I was always getting penance for it
and having to sit in after school. I didn't mind this at all since
I preferred it to going home and, as far as my mother was concerned, she would have been happy for me to stay in school
twenty-four hours a day since it was run by the priests. Finally,
I overdid it. Talking was always my thing. I can't help it. I
just have to talk to people. But, naturally, the teachers didn't
see it that way so I was told that if I didn't leave they'd have
to expel me.

I couldn't tell my mother for about a week and I'd go out as
if I were going to school and spend my time in Port of Spain
looking for jobs with other boys who had left.

The only job that interested me was going to sea—it offered
total escape from home—and that was difficult as I wore short
pants and didn't look a day older than my fourteen years. Every
day I would go down to the docks in the hope of being taken
on board a ship as a cabin boy. The docks were really pretty
ramshackle, with broken-down wooden sheds around the wharves,
dilapidated jetties jutting and crumbling into the muddy water
and dozens of decrepit old salts who would never sail again, but
who hung around constantly in a dream that their ship was coming
to take them away. But to me it was beautiful. There was all that
bustle of great things afoot : dredgers clearing the silt washed in
by the Orinoco; schooners from small islands bringing fruit,
sweet potatoes and poultry into the port; ships bringing in
bauxite from the developing mines in British Guiana for transfer

to the bigger ocean-going cargo vessels; yachts owned by rich American tourists anchoring off shore; rowing boats flitting like insects amongst the bigger craft. . . .

I would stand on the edge of the dock longingly watching the boats sailing off through the gateway to the bay, formed by a group of little islands, to the sparkling blue sea beyond. If you kept your gaze high it was a picturesque scene. Even the name of the entrance to the bay had a romantic sound—Gran Boca del Toro. And the exotic stories the old seamen used to tell would fire my imagination still more. They would sit in the shade of the crumbling sheds in their tattered clothes rambling on and on with faraway eyes to boys like me who could never hear enough. Everything they talked about was something you didn't have, something desirable : other countries, other ports, money, clothes, skyscrapers, underground trains, snowstorms, luxury liners, Big Ben. . . .

Eventually, in desperation, I would take to cadging the use of a rowing boat, or hiring it with the little money I won at some game or other, and rowing out to every ship that entered the harbour to climb aboard and ask for a job. It was always a frustrating and fruitless waste of energy. They either wanted an experienced sailor, or they demanded money to take you on as a beginner. Some wouldn't want black boys on their books. Others would say they'd cabled ashore for people and you'd have to go to the shipping office—where they'd always say someone else had already been signed up.

After a while I had to tell my mother I'd been kicked out of school. She was horrified and went to see the priests and somehow arranged for me to go back. But I didn't. I was fed up with school and insisted on having a job. I was completely immovable and my mother found there was nothing, for once, that she could do about it. It was the first serious decision I'd taken.

From then on my mother and I would have a daily pantomime. I would get up in the morning and prepare to go out. She would say : 'Where you going?' I would reply : 'Down by the docks.' She would say : 'You can't do this—working with your hands. You got to have a decent job.' I would say nothing and leave for the docks. My mother would have been delighted had I become a priest, a doctor, or a lawyer. She loved white people and these were the jobs they were identified with. The idea of my doing any sort of manual labour was anathema to her.

I remember one day a sailor at the docks was trying to sell
a shirt, the way sailors would sell lots of things they picked up
from their trips. It was a marvellous American two-tone shirt
in brown, and he wanted three dollars for it. I never wanted
anything so much as I wanted that shirt and I asked my mother
for the money. I knew she had a lot of money in the house because,
apart from her obeah activities, she ran a sue-sue. A sue-sue
is a kind of bank into which a number of people will pay a
weekly sum and each, periodically, will get the whole sum for
a given week. It was one way to get a large sum of bread if
you needed it, and nobody missed the weekly contribution.
Around this scene you also got a lot of other people wanting
loans—a dollar for a rum—and paying back with interest. Or,
maybe, a guy would get arrested for stealing or being drunk and
disorderly and need thirty dollars bail. The sue-sue holder was in
a position to produce this sort of sum and charge ten per cent
for it. There were all sorts of angles once you had the capital
and my mother was doing very well out of it. But she wouldn't
give me three dollars for the shirt and so I decided I'd have to
do some manual work for it.

I went to the Savannah where there was usually some sort
of work going and asked the groundsman if he had anything
I could do. He did and he set me to work rolling the cricket
pitches at a rate of five dollars a day. It wasn't overpaid, since
rolling with huge, heavy rollers in temperatures ranging from
85-90 degrees Fahrenheit can be really tough work and there
were a lot of pitches.

I had my shirt off and was sweating away heaving the roller
back and forth when a neighbour passed and spread the word
to my mother. Suddenly I heard this terrible screaming: 'Oh
God! Oh God!' and I looked up and there she was standing
way off holding her head and yelling: 'All I do for you! I
give you everything you want and this is what you do to me!
This is what you bring me to!'

In the same breath she tore a roll of notes from her bosom.

'Three dollars you want!' she screamed. And peeling off the
bills, she flung them on the grass and went off screaming the
injustice of it and my lack of feeling.

Really I should have carried on rolling, but I got very weak
at the sight of the money and I pulled on my shirt, picked up
the bills and went off to the docks to make my purchase. The

sailor had probably bought it in a fifty-cent store, but I seldom had anything to show off and I was very happy with my three dollars-worth.

Shortly after this I took a job as an errand boy at a department store in Port of Spain, working for five dollars a week. It was terribly poorly paid and in no time at all sheer necessity pushed me to work out a simple fiddle. Apart from jobs like cleaning shelves, it was the errand boys' task to wait for the cry of 'Cash!' from the salesmen and then run like hell carrying the shopper's money to the cashier in another part of the store and return with the change and counterfoil for the customer. Accounting in those days was not what it is today. In fact it hardly existed and it was the simplest matter to tear off the counterfoil on the way to the cashier, pocket the purchaser's note and the bill, pro-duce the change myself and return with it and the counterfoil without ever reaching the cashier's desk. As soon as I could, I would withdraw to the toilet and flush my collection of bills down the lavatory while I gleefully counted the day's takings. One of the first things I did with my supplementary income, was, for some unaccountable reason, to buy a new look dress for my mother.

However, I couldn't risk doing this with too much regularity and after about six months I found the sheer economic drag of the job was too much. Travelling, eating, new white shirts, the whole respectable ballyhoo of having a job . . . the money went nowhere and I began to look around for something that paid more.

It was while I was looking that a Portuguese shopkeeper asked me if I ever heard from my father and then gave me his address in the island of St Kitts. So I wrote to tell him I had grown up and left school and would like to see him. To my surprise I had a letter back by return of post enclosing money to buy clothes preparatory to visiting him. My mother was very pleased. Look-ing back, I think she felt in the depths of her mind that if I went to see him she'd be following after. Anyway, she took the money and bought me an air ticket to St Kitts in place of the clothes.

My mother and some neighbours hired a car to take me the eighteen miles to the airport. They were all crying like hell, which I couldn't understand as I was so very happy to be getting out of the island.

The old plane was completely full and I was terribly excited and feeling very grown up at being completely on my own. The actual experience of flying left me feeling very cool, though. It wasn't any more than a first taxi or tramcar ride. I got much more kick from a motor boat. The aeroplane touched down in a number of islands and I had the impression it couldn't stay up in the air for too long at a time.

My mother was not efficient enough to let my father know I was coming. She'd simply given me a couple of rum bottle labels which gave the address of his shop and I showed these to the immigration men when we landed and they directed me to a taxi.

St Kitts seemed like a small town compared with Trinidad and the houses were smaller and the people looked poorer, all walking around in bare feet. But I was drinking it all in as the beginning of a new life. I just walked in on my father and he recognised me from all those years ago. To me he didn't look like any of the descriptions I'd heard. I saw a large, round man whose muscular body had put on fat with the years; a good-looking, hefty guy who was a rich man. I had no emotion about him. And I never did get to know him.

He stood and looked at me in the near-deserted bar, and then he came around the counter, looking at me and saying to someone standing with his drink at the bar. 'This is my son—I knew he was going to come.'

We exchanged a few pleasantries and then he picked up my suitcase and took me up to my room, telling me I should have waited a bit as he was getting it fixed up and then I would have had a really nice homecoming. That didn't worry me. The room wasn't at all bad: small, but adequate, with a table opposite the bed and a water basin and with a window overlooking a neighbour's back yard.

My father had a number of liquor stores all over the island. They call them rum shops in the West Indies and you drink in them. This one, the Rising Sun in Market Street, Basseterre, was very popular. I soon knew all about it since the next day he put me to work serving over the counter. I got board and lodging, but no wages—they were never mentioned. I felt secure, though, with the thought that everything was mine. After all, he was my father.

During the three months I worked at the shop I saw him only at intervals. I would sweep it out at seven a.m. for opening at seven-thirty and I'd work through the day until nine at night. There was a back yard where local musicians would play under a lean-to and the drinkers would listen and clap and get drunk and wild. People don't go in for sophisticated talk in the rum shops. They'd come in, swallow their eight-cent rums standing at the counter under the shadow of the giant rum casks, and end up very aggressive. There were fights all over the place.

These were the only people I got to know in the island. Sometimes I'd eat with one of my cousins in the shop, but I never knew who my father's friends were and he never introduced me to people of my own age. He owned property and racehorses, but the most I ever saw of the horses was when they passed the shop on their way to the track.

A number of whores came into the bar. They were much older than me—in their twenties—but I was growing up and some of them began to get very friendly with me. Since my father left the whole running of the store to me, I began to take money out of the till for beer and entertainment. After all, he didn't pay me and I didn't see why I shouldn't have a few dollars. I began going out with these ladies after I'd finished my chores at the bar and my father got to hear about it. Apparently he took a dim view of it, although he never said anything to me.

At the end of three months he told me he wanted to go to America for an operation and I should go back to Trinidad. I knew there was no question of any operation and, in any case, there was no reason why I should leave even if there were. But he was insistent and said he wanted to close the shop down while he was away. It was all an excuse to get rid of me. I think he must have been fed up that I was running a bit wild and that two of my lady friends were old flames of his.

I said I didn't want to go back to Trinidad, but he was adamant and bought me a ticket. He also gave me a hundred dollars—the first and only payment for three months' work. He was my father and I went to him and ended up being employed by him from my first day, working long hours, seven days a week. I expected to go out and meet people, have some social life, but I never did. I wouldn't treat a son of mine that way.

Back in Trinidad I told them he'd gone to America for an operation and I spent two months walking around looking for a job. My mother disapproved of everything I tried and when I

worked for the peppermint man, she would scream hysterically
at me on the street.

His name was Da Silva and he had this sweetie scene going.
He would boil sugar in a copper pot until it reached the right
consistency, lay it out on marble slabs, roll it into pieces while it
was still hot, hook the pieces over a couple of nails on the wall
and start pulling them. They would keep falling and he would
keep pulling and I would be cutting the strips into little sweet
lengths. He was a Latin-looking type and very jolly. He had his
family of four children helping him and, at the age of twenty-four,
that was all he wanted to do—pull sweeties. I enjoyed his company and the atmosphere of his place, but, even though he was a
white man, my mother couldn't stand that I was working with
my hands that way and began spreading such terrible stories
about the orgies we were supposed to be having amongst the
sweets that I left in embarrassment.

I made a little money after that helping to organise the ring
games during the horse-racing season at the Savannah. You'd
rope off a box acquired from a Chinese grocery, place some coins
on top and invite people to circle them by throwing little rings
made from electric wire. I sold the rings, five for a shilling, and
picked them off the table. It was completely illegal, of course, but
the police usually turned a blind eye, presumably because they
were getting a rake-off. The danger was from hooligans who
were always fighting all around with razors and cutlasses, and
upsetting everything.

Trinidad in those days was full of eruptive violence. I remember seeing one guy slash off a coconut vendor's hand with a cutlass during some argument. The hand was lying on the ground
beside me and I swear it moved. The police came rushing up
to grab witnesses. One of them caught me and said he wanted me
to go to court to tell what I'd seen. When I told him the hand
had moved, he changed his mind and wouldn't have me as a wit-
ness at any price.

Often the violence was allied with sheer lunacy. I knew a
young guy in Belmont who walked around with two toy guns
strapped to his side, saying 'Stick 'em up' to everyone. And everyone laughed and raised his hands, crying : 'Bob, you are a great
guy.' One day when he was eighteen he said to someone 'Stick
'em up' and the guy told him to shut up and Bob just shot him
dead with the real pistols he'd substituted for the toy ones.

Then there was my friend Gold Teeth, a big Trinidadian who thought he was a cowboy and went around trying to hold up clubs. On one occasion the manager of a club turned him away and Gold Teeth took out an iron bolt and smashed it on his feet. When the manager doubled up in agony, yelling about his feet, Gold Teeth grinned at him and said: 'No, it's waggon wheels.'

Perhaps the craziest of all was the Indian who used to drive an imaginary car all around Port of Spain. He would even buy petrol with the pump attendants humouring him and pretending to fill up and occasionally he bought a newspaper and flung it through the make-believe window of the make-believe car into the make-believe back seat. I even knew him to get fighting mad when someone leaned on the space where his car was supposed to be parked. 'Get your damned carcase off my car,' he yelled.

These people were supposed to be driven mad by obeah and they were not uncommon in Trinidad.

All this time my mother kept telling me to go back to my father and eventually she got the money together and sent me back. Once again he didn't know I was coming and I just turned up at his door. This time he drove me straight to a hotel and left me there, saying he'd pay for my room for one week. He didn't want me in his house or business, so I went around the island and found myself a job in the Public Works Department as a time keeper. They were a bit surprised in the Department as they knew I was Michael de Freitas and my father was rich. However, I was quite happy with the biggest wage I'd ever had—about 14 dollars a week. It wouldn't pay the hotel bill, of course, but the proprietor didn't worry because of my rich family. After a month he started asking for some money and I just learned to say no.

'Don't ask me,' I would say. 'I didn't book in.'

Everything was fine for a while until my boss got arrested for fraud. I had nothing to do with it but I lost my job, and my father, who was afraid I would get arrested and disgrace him, put me on a plane for Trinidad, telling me to get out before I landed in gaol. I paid that hotel bill myself five years later.

On my return to Trinidad I discovered I finally had the job I'd always wanted. I'd registered with the Norwegian shipping office during my previous stay and now they offered me a job as a galley boy on a small freighter carrying bauxite from British Guiana to Canada. The ship was named *Polycrest* and it was from Christianssand in Norway. It had a very exotic crew: the officers were Norwegian and the crew was composed of eight Spaniards, two Frenchmen, four Germans and a Trinidadian cook.

I went aboard with the Trinidadian and someone from the shipping office and handed my passport to the Chief Officer. There was no work until the morning, as I had been taken on as galley boy, and so I wandered around the deck watching the sailors preparing the ship for departure and then hung over the rail to see the lights of Port of Spain dwindling away as we put out to sea in a gentle Caribbean swell.

I never knew what my duties as galley boy would have been because I was terribly sick almost from the moment I woke up in my cabin next day and they eventually had to switch me with the engine boy. I seemed to be sick for a lifetime, but once I came round I enjoyed the engine room. I wiped oil off the floor, filled oil cans and disposed of dirty rags. It was a swinging job. The Trinidadian cook and I were the only West Indians aboard, but the rest of the crew spoke English and we got along pretty well.

I adjusted to the life very quickly once my sickness was over and I was delighted with my wages of around four dollars a day —a sum which even adults didn't earn in Trinidad. How many days from here to Canada, I kept asking. Every day was helping to make me a fortune.

Once we got to Canada I didn't have much time to see anything, but I remember the beer taverns were cleaner than anything I'd seen and the ice cream was wonderful. We took a cargo of dynamite back to the West Indies and I was paid off with about 90 dollars and began the impatient wait for my next ship.

I waited about four weeks and then I was taken on another Norwegian vessel, a tanker, going to West Africa. This trip gave me the first view of the home of my ancestors—Ghana, Nigeria, the Ivory Coast—the land where the slaves came from. And I didn't think much of it. I couldn't help contrasting West Africa with Canada. All the people I saw there were poor and black, while in Canada they were rich and white. Canada was a big place full of people working; Africa was full of people begging. It certainly corroborated my mother's view. Pretty was Canada— and there was no beauty in Africa for me.

Between voyages I stayed with my mother and stepfather. My mother was very pleased about my new life as I was able to give her a lot of money and presents, but my stepfather dis-

approved of the irregularity of the work and was constantly telling me I should get a steady job like in the police force.

'You'd be a sergeant in no time with your colour,' he'd tell me.
The colour thing went on and on.

When I was about sixteen I had this very nice looking black
girl friend, Gloria. I was friendly with her brother and I thought
her family nice people. I was courting her like mad and one day
I summoned up enough courage to invite her over to our house.
She had been playing tennis and she arrived prettily dressed in
white tennis blouse and shorts. We were sitting chatting when my
mother came back from shopping and began behaving in her
very icy way. I introduced them and my mother went about her
business, glancing at us from time to time, listening to our conversation, trying to pretend she wasn't.

It was quite obvious that I liked Gloria very much, I suppose,
and I was asking her what she would like me to bring back for
her on my next trip to Africa. Her brother was a seaman, too,
and had once brought his mother some crocodile skin bags from
Africa, and Gloria was saying something about how she would
love to have a similar bag when my mother suddenly went quite
hysterical. She started yelling abuse at Gloria and ordered her
from the house in an incredible outburst.

Gloria was terribly upset and we both left. I took her home
and that was more or less the end of our friendship. Nobody
would want to have that happen twice.

When I got back I confronted my mother and asked her what
she meant by her behaviour.

'You're not having any black girls in this house!' she cried.
'You're not going through the trouble I went through.'

'What's that got to do with Gloria?' I asked.

'I try to show you what's good and you can't take your nose
out of the gutter,' she ranted. 'Always running around with black
people—and now you want black women. I heard her asking
you for bags.'

Small wonder that I took to staying out late with boys of my
age, or slightly older. We would drink beers by the sea and talk
about our voyages. But when I got home my stepfather started
telling me I was staying out too late and had to be in earlier. I
was amazed and tried to explain that I was no longer a boy, that
I was now a seaman, used to living my own life and that I would
shortly be off again.

'There can't be two men in this house,' he said.

My mother took his side completely and, since if I had stayed I would have had to fight him, I left the house.

I went to live with some Indian neighbours. They were a huge family of twenty-one, all living in three little houses on their smallholding. The second eldest son, Sampath, was one of my greatest friends. He was five years older than me and, in fact, I idolised him. He was very beautiful, muscular and agile, and extremely kind and loyal. As one of the eldest of the family, he had a bed to himself, but he insisted on giving it to me and slept on the floor himself. I lived with them for about a week before I went to sea again and they treated me royally. They made interesting curries and sometimes killed a goat for feast days.

As far as my mother was concerned this was the end. She had always forbidden me to speak to them since 'coolies' were the lowest form of life—lower even than the niggers. There couldn't be anything lower than going back to the earth—and they planted corn and kept goats. She wouldn't speak to me until after my next trip.

I left them to make the trip every West Indian waits for—the chance to visit Britain.

The job had started as a shuttle service between Trinidad and the South American mainland, but the engine fouled up and it was decided the vessel should be sent to England to dry dock.

England was home in the mind of every small boy in the West Indies when I was growing up. Land of hope and glory. We sang that song as little boys with the greatest fervour. I was thrilled with the prospect of seeing the mother country. I didn't know then that it was the first step on the road to disillusion.

3

My first view of England had all the enchantment of the exotic Christmas cards I'd sometimes seen as a small child.

It was snowing as we approached the estuary of the Mersey on our way to dock for repairs in Liverpool. It was cold, too, but I hardly noticed. All I could do was gaze in an agony of excitement at the cosy, white-topped houses and the coastline also blanketed white. I had all the experienced sailors grinning as I demanded constantly: 'What's that? And that? And that over there. . . ?'

'England,' they roared, laughing. 'Fish and chips . . . black and tan. . . .' And they went below to keep warm in the mess hall while they waited for the clearing of the ship.

I stayed on deck, ignoring the fact that I was turning blue, studying the giant ocean-going liners at anchor, the ferry boats criss-crossing from bank to bank, the people I could make out on the shore. In that moment I felt I had arrived. I was home, in the mother country and the days of hanging around the waterfront of Trinidad waiting for jobs were gone for ever.

I suppose my experience that night was no more than the anticlimax sailors so often feel throughout the world, but for me it seemed to set the tone for all that was to come in England.

We took a taxi to Lime Street where we understood all the action was. The cabbie drove and drove until it seemed at one time we must be driving right across the country. He put us down near the Adelphi Hotel and charged us £5 without batting an eyelid. Nothing much seemed to be happening and we asked a passer-by for the nearest night club. He looked at us blankly and shrugged. There was no action in Lime Street. We crowded into the nearest pub, but the landlord was already calling time and he wouldn't sell us a bottle to take away. Outside, the snow was turning to dirty, freezing slush, and had already lost its charm.

By the time we sailed on to Cardiff for dry docking I was sick with colds and fever, and I left the boat and booked in at the seamen's hostel. I was on pay with board and accommodation as long as I remained sick.

After a couple of weeks recuperation I decided to come off the sick list and make the most of being in Britain by looking around for a job. I had soon got to know a lot of young coloured boys of my age in Cardiff and they told me to apply for a job with the British Merchant Navy Office and gave me the address. These boys had already been to sea or were about to go, following in the footsteps of their fathers.

The office was in the basement of a huge building in the docks. I went there next day and saw the shipmaster. He was directing the black and white seamen who went in there all through the day and there seemed to be so much action that I felt I was sure to get a job with no trouble. I gave him my passport and he took other particulars and sent me into a committee room for an interview.

There were three men sitting behind a big table : typical nice, kind, fatherly, upper-crust Englishmen. I sat on a chair across the desk from them and told them I wanted a job on a British ship. They asked about my experience on Norwegian vessels and told me it was possible I could be placed. Would you like to go back to the West Indies as a d.b.s. (displaced British seaman) they asked me. This meant working one's passage to get home. No, I told them in some surprise. I didn't want to go back home. I wanted a job. They regarded me gravely. All right, their spokesman said, if I wanted a job on a British ship I would have to go to the mercantile school in Cardiff and get a ticket to prove that I was capable.

Before I went to the mercantile school later that day, I talked to an old West Indian seaman I knew and he told me that whatever else I did to make sure I was very polite to the instructor.

The instructor turned out to be kind, in fact. He asked me all about the ships I'd sailed on and what I'd done on them and then he set me certain tests.

B

The school was beautiful—a wonderful place fitted with steering wheel, compass and all the other things one finds on board ship. I could have stayed there all day. The instructor had me read the compass, tie certain knots, steer a ship, while he watched every move I made. The Norwegians trained their men well and I went through it all without any trouble so that he seemed quite pleased when I'd finished and wrote out a certificate for me without any hesitation.

Next day I went back to the Merchant Navy Office, expecting the committee men to be pleased and thinking, 'I'm on.'

I was ushered into the room and handed them the ticket which they looked at for a minute or two before the spokesman said they could probably find me a job in an engine room. I replied that I didn't want that; I'd been working on deck as a deck boy and was applying for a job as a junior ordinary seaman.

At this, one of them said : 'You might have to wait a while. We do have ships with all-coloured crews—West Indians, Arabs and that—but you might have to wait.'

'I'm not fussy about being on one of those,' I said. 'Any ship will do me.'

'I'm sorry,' the spokesman said then. 'But it won't be possible for you to work on deck on an ordinary British ship. You see we don't mix crews on deck.'

I was stunned. Looking back, I realised my young friends in Cardiff understood the sort of jobs open to them, like working in the galley or the engine room, but I didn't know there was any sort of bar and I was quite upset when I found out. I didn't try to argue with the committee. I was only sixteen and I simply thought, well that's what's happening here. I left the office and spoke to the old West Indian seaman about it and his reaction was : 'Well, this is England.' He dismissed the whole incident with that comment as if it was to be expected and was not terribly important. But it was important and it still is. This 'whites only' policy is still in practice with the British Merchant Marine.

Thus it was that the mother country threw me back on the mercy of the Norwegian Merchant Navy. I went to them with my union card immediately and they registered me as a deck boy on their first available boat without any questions whatever.

It's hardly surprising that I'm very fond of Norwegians. They employed me for years when the British wouldn't and I feel I

grew up with them more than in Trinidad. I speak fluent Norwegian and I still have many Norwegian friends. Colour prejudice doesn't seem to exist for them.

At this time and at other times to come I lived in Tiger Bay—
the dock area. The Bay was a world of its own, cut off from the
rest of the city. A black world. It swarmed with West Indians,
Arabs, Somalis, Pakistanis and a legion of half caste children. In
its food stores you could buy cassavas and red peppers and in the
restaurants you could eat curries and rice dishes just like those
in the West Indies.

The city's black people, who mostly worked in the docks, were
the sweetest people I've ever met in Britain. They had a real
friendliness. Everyone seemed to be married to everyone else's
sister and they'd all sit on the doorsteps of the elegant, dilapidated
old houses chatting and exchanging greetings. Whenever I
appeared they would make me feel completely at home.

'Hello Michael, how long you going to stay?' they would ask,
or even, 'How long you going to be home?'

I usually lived with a half caste family who cooked Trinidadian
food and I would spend my time talking, going to the Friday
night dance at the solitary dance hall and watching the street
gambling. This was illegal, of course, but even the policemen had
grown up in Tiger Bay and when they saw a crowd standing in a
circle they'd know a couple of men were in the middle shooting
dice and they'd stroll in the other direction. They very rarely
broke up a game.

There were a lot of old timers, old sea salts, in the Bay and
when I sat around chatting with them they'd always tell me the
same thing—to stay with the Norwegians and not get mixed up
with British ships because there was no future on them for a
black man; he couldn't get anywhere.

For much the same reason they seldom crossed the canal which
formed a frontier between Tiger Bay and the rest of Cardiff.
They preferred to stay in the family atmosphere away from the
cold prejudice they met in the white world beyond.

Prejudice is not an easy thing to define. If you try, people
usually say you are hypersensitive, or you have a chip on your
shoulder, or some bullshit like that. But you know all about it
if you're its victim. Like many other black people from Tiger Bay,
I've had the experience of going up into the white town, standing in a bar and calling for a half pint and having the barman

look straight at me and through me and serve everyone else until there was nothing to do but leave.

Not that white people ever left Tiger Bay alone. They were always driving across the canal bridge at night and slumming it along Bute Street. They had the idea that the Bay was a den of vice and violence and they wanted to add a little spice to their lives.

I don't think I ever saw a fight in Tiger Bay. All I remember are the smiling families on the doorsteps and the beautiful black children playing everywhere.

I spent the next few years on Norwegian boats travelling around the world. The first one I took out of Cardiff proved to be a very valuable part of my apprenticeship. It was just about the oldest Norwegian vessel in existence: a forty-three-year-old freight steamer with its parts riveted together rather than welded the way modern ships are. It was so ramshackle that I didn't really want to travel two inches on it; I wanted to get off just as soon as I got on. The trouble was I had no money and though you are normally allowed to refuse up to three vessels when you're on the list, I had no choice but to take the first that came along.

But the compensation was that with the tiny crew on such a small, old vessel, the training was so much better. On deck each man had to do virtually everything—drive winches, load, un-load. . . .

We were going to Spain to take up a cargo of pit props and I remember that when we were winching up the lines to begin the voyage, the vibration of the winches had the thin deck plates shaking so badly I felt sure they were going to fall apart. My fears were only too well grounded. When we were right in the middle of the Bay of Biscay the side of the ship fell off. There was a fairly heavy swell and suddenly we heard this almighty wrenching sound and there was one of the plates of the hull just hanging off, flap-ping, leaving a gaping hole about ten feet by six on the water line. The sea came gushing into the hatches before we even knew what was happening.

The Norwegians, as I've said, are very good seamen and the skipper remained impressively cool. He got the pumps going and used the ballast tanks to turn the ship over on its safe side. At a thirty-degree angle it was impossible to walk on the deck and we were scrambling around in our lifebelts, all secured with ropes like mountaineers. The skipper dealt with the hole by having us fit two huge planks over it and sandwiching a thick layer of cement between them. It was a clever and adequate remedy and enabled us to limp into Lisbon for repairs.

From then on I got steady promotion : junior ordinary seaman, senior ordinary seaman and able seaman as I made trips around Europe, to Canada, the Persian Gulf, the West Indies, everywhere.

There was only one time that I regretted the life and that was during a massive storm which I didn't expect us to survive. We were returning to Norway from the Gulf in a tanker of about 14,000 tons and had been sixty days at sea without shore leave when this terrible storm hit us in the Irish Sea. The waves piled up fifty or sixty feet high so that the ship seemed to be a puny thing in a valley with great moving mountains all around that appeared likely to fall and crush us at every moment. The sea was a very terrible and cruel being, crashing against us constantly. It smashed plates and knocked in a side of the ship. It tore one of the lifeboats away. It really began to destroy us.

I was one of four men amidships and we were marooned there, cut off from the rest of the ship and the crew. The sea was pouring over the decks and it carried off the catwalk connecting us to the aft deck and the crew's quarters. The four of us took turns on the midships bridge to keep a constant lookout. We were marooned for three days, during which time I had an average of two hours sleep a night. My first watch lasted more than twenty hours and the officer with us was on his feet for twenty-four. We used the ship's hospital for sleeping in and opened whatever tins were about, since we were cut off from the galleys. I've never been so sick of sardines in my life.

They kept trying to throw us a line from aft so that we could haul over a rope by it and make ourselves a connecting bridge, but the sea never gave us a chance. We watched our life raft being lifted off by the waves and go floating away. I really began to think the sea was going to get us and there was absolutely nothing we could do about it.

We hung on in a state of near exhaustion until finally at the end of the third day the storm passed as if it had just been testing us and we staggered into Bergen a beaten wreck. No town had ever seemed so beautiful as Bergen at that time.

Between voyages I went back to Trinidad and I felt great about the clothes I had and the fact that I could buy beer for all my friends. But at home it was the same old story. My mother and stepfather were delighted while I was away because I was sending them anything from 50 to 100 dollars every month. But once I got back and the money stopped, my stepfather would start asking how long I thought I was going to stay and when I was going to get a regular job. I wouldn't keep money long during these spells because my reaction as a sailor was to drink with what I had left and to share it with my friends, living a rather easy life.

It was to get away during one of these jobless periods that I borrowed some money and took an immigrant boat from Trinidad to England.

It was a European vessel with conditions worse than any troopship. The fare was £65 with no questions asked and we were packed twenty-two in a cabin. Everybody was so sick that the mess for the first few days was unimaginable. Everywhere I looked people were turning green and thinking, as one does, that they were never going to recover. I didn't get sick and I was able to help a bit, but I couldn't stand the cabins and I slept on deck on a coil of rope.

When they weren't feeling too ill to think about anything, these people were full of illusions, which they used to talk about. Ninety per cent of them intended to work and study something in England. They thought it was going to be wonderful and that they were going to make something of themselves at last. I knew they were never going to make it. I'd look at them in their light gaberdines, straw hats and torn shoes and I'd say that it wasn't all that great, that they wouldn't find a job just like that and that rents were high, and insurance and tax and the cost of living. I'd tell them about colour prejudice and they wouldn't believe me. They couldn't understand why I'd be going to England again if it was like that. I didn't bother to explain I'd be heading straight for the Norwegian Merchant Navy Office.

But the sadness I felt about their forlorn hopes was partially offset by the sheer pleasure of being on a boat with hundreds of my own people. There was a ship's band and sometimes some of the Trinidadians who were coming to England to be musicians would play calypsos and Latin American music. What with the crowds, the music and the drink, the trip became very exciting. West Indian women, like any others, become very hot in the constrained atmosphere of a ship and I would say that particular boat was just about the biggest floating whorehouse in the world. There were young women let loose from their families for the first time, others having a last fling before joining their husbands in Britain. The trip had its compensations.

The boat went to Genoa and then the passengers were taken by train overland to London. My final memory of all those hopeful people is of the chaos they faced at Victoria Station where British Railways decreed that their luggage should be put in one big pile on the platform. The pickpockets and petty thieves well knew the routine . . . take a platform ticket and just pick up any case.

4

When I was about nineteen, I made another trip to Africa and smoked my first marijuana.

The boat had anchored in the estuary of a river between Lagos and a village on the opposite bank. There were several West Indians in the crew and we were going to take a steel band ashore. We knew if we went into Lagos we would probably spend quite a bit of money and so we went to the village instead, just to get our land legs.

We started to play on the outskirts of the village. I was shaking maraccas and the others were playing drums and other instruments. In no time we were surrounded by delighted Nigerians, who began dancing and leading us to clearings amongst the mud huts, setting us up in front of their little shops and at intersections in the dirt tracks which were the streets. We really swang for quite a long time, taking a breath now and then when they brought us fruit juices or we purchased a few beers.

In the middle of the dancing and general gaiety, this little old lady suddenly turned up with a brown paper parcel which she presented to us as if it were a gift of gold and diamonds. We opened it up and it was something like half a pound of pot.

There was a big, happy distribution scene with all the men filling pipes with it and everyone smoking merrily away—including the old lady. The band went with an extra swing from then on. The pot had very little effect on me, but I thought it would be fun to take some back to Trinidad and the villagers gave us quite a supply.

Back home, in the back yard of the house where I'd planted corn as a young boy, I now sowed my first crop of marijuana. It grew beautifully and in no time the trees were bigger than me— splendid enough to give the average magistrate apoplexy. My friends flocked to the back yard and we all had some very happy times. It seemed so harmless to me that I never thought about it being against the law. I'd drunk socially from an early age and watched other people get drunk and want to fight and start vomiting all over the place. With pot smoking I saw them, instead, sitting quietly and peacefully talking about all sorts of interesting things they might otherwise have ignored. For myself, I normally talked a lot without any kind of drug, but when I smoked I found I would listen to what other people were saying rather than doing all the talking myself.

So I was surprised to learn much later that after I left someone got word that the police were on their way and my friends ripped up the trees and burned them.

The official attitude towards pot in Trinidad is comic. It grows wild there anyway, but they think it's a dangerous drug and won't admit there's any in the island. If the authorities do hear of a tree, they surreptitiously send out a dozen detectives to track it down.

If I were president of an independent country, I would legalise drugs and get a sensible approach to them. They're beginning to understand in Britain that marijuana is not habit-forming like tobacco and alcohol and is less injurious to health. The British approach to heroin—allowing addicts to have it on prescription —is very sensible. A man attached to heroin is a sick man and should be treated as such. Force him to go among criminals to get it and you'll make him a criminal too.

Japan . . . Canada . . . Africa . . . I got almost dizzy going around the world, until one day I got off a vessel in Virginia, USA and had a letter from my mother saying my father had died of double pneumonia. I felt hurt for a few minutes, but by that evening I was knocking back rum in the bars and had forgotten all about it. As I've said, I didn't know the man.

I don't think this is all that heartless. I was never very close to him. It would be nice to spout some kind of shit about the wonderful parents I had, but it would pain me more to lie like that. My father wasn't evil towards me, just thoughtless. And my mother never could behave well. Even when she first came to

England, when I had money and wanted her to respect her age and herself and forget Trinidad where hustling was a way of life, she wouldn't take a bit of notice. I kept telling her to cool it, but the only thing that interested her was to surround herself with white prostitutes and rent property for brothels. . . .

During my time at sea I had plenty of opportunity to learn what a white-orientated world it is—including the inevitable scene in South Africa.

We were on an oil trip from Rio round the Cape to the Gulf and we docked at Durban to take on provisions. I went ashore with a Trinidadian friend who would pass for white and a big blond Norwegian. The bars were divided into Indian and European. We went into an Indian bar first and they wouldn't serve us because we were the wrong colour mixture. We went into a European bar next and they refused us service for the same reason. So we bought a few bottles and sat by the roadside near one of the long beaches, away from the built-up area, drinking. There were plenty of other groups sitting around enjoying themselves. But no blacks with whites.

In a very short time we were arrested by a policeman, who simply took us in without any explanation. At the station we were placed in the cells—my two apparently white shipmates in one, me in another. My friends protested at this and were told to shut up. I said we were doing no harm at all and was told to shut up. That was the stock answer to everything.

After a while an officer came from the ship and said it was ready to sail. He was allowed to pay a fine on our behalf and take us away with him. A lot of the crew said we were very lucky to get off so lightly and that we had been very stupid.

Discrimination has many shades. In Canada and the United States I found it slightly different.

About the time I was twenty-one, I was made boatswain of a Norwegian vessel. This meant that as chief petty officer I had general supervision of the crew and was responsible for keeping the ship in good order. It also meant that I was the liaison officer with the foreman of the dock crew who would come aboard to arrange the unloading of the cargo.

In places like Toronto and New York, the foreman would come aboard and ask for the boatswain. When I turned up he would say: 'Where's the bosun? it's the bosun I want.' And I would reply: 'I'm the bosun.' At that, he would make some crack and go looking elsewhere as if I were joking. They just wouldn't believe that a black man could hold the position. At first this annoyed me, but eventually I got used to it.

One of the foremen once asked me how I got along with the Norwegian crew and when I said I got along with them very well, he said, in some surprise: 'Oh well, you speak their language,' as if that could be the only possible reason. Another foreman was so fascinated that he took me for a drink, hoping to discover that I didn't really get on with the crew at all. He finished by declaring that he just didn't think it was right for white men to be working under a black man. But he couldn't begin to tell me why.

At that point one simply says: 'Have another drink.' There's no point in arguing.

5

I came off ships because I met the woman I married. I was about twenty-five years old and before her I'd never shown or felt any great interest in women, although I had slept with a few. I'd worked on ships since I was a boy and they were what I really cared about. I had that same sort of feeling for ships that some people who can drive extremely well have about cars. I understood them. I could rig them beautifully. I could handle them in rough weather. They had been my life.

I met Desirée at a West Indian party in London while I was on a few days' shore leave. It was a birthday celebration for one of a group of people I usually visited, and it was just like any other West Indian party. It was held in a small room in a rather dilapidated house in Latimer Road with a lot of noise, a lot of dancing and everyone getting drunk.

The people were very nice. There was Doris, whose party it was and there was her brother Clarence whom I admired very much because he was tall and slim, strong and violent and had great success with women. West Indians are very fond of their pricks and like to talk a lot about their conquests. I had no tales to tell because I never had any conquests, so I would just listen to Clarence and be amused. He gave me the feeling he could have any woman he wanted by some sort of magic.

In the middle of the evening, amidst all the music and laughter, this tiny and terribly pretty woman appeared. She had olive-brown skin and a very shapely body and her bright, intelligent

eyes exuded an air which combined pride and gaiety. I saw
Clarence looking at her and I asked him who she was. He said:
'I don't know, but I'm going to find out.' I told him not to bother
and he asked why not. 'Because I want her,' I said. I remember
him laughing and finding it very strange, because I never usually
wanted women.

Later I asked her to dance, which was rather stupid because I
couldn't dance. It had never been my scene. But we moved
around the floor and I talked about my ship and finally got
around to asking her if she would come out with me next day.
She said she wasn't sure if she could as she had a child to look
after. I thought at first she was a nurse taking care of someone's
child and I said: 'Well bring it along.' She said all right, but
something in her attitude made me ask whose child it was and
she said, 'Mine'. I told her I'd like to see the child anyway and
gave her the name of the Norwegian Hotel in Lancaster Gate
where I was staying.

I have often wondered why I pursued that relationship and I
think the child had quite a bit to do with it. She was a two-year-
old girl and the father was a Trinidadian Desirée had known
when she first came to England. This was quite normal to me. In
Trinidad two thirds of the births are illegitimate; marriage isn't
the institution it is in this country. Anyway, when Desirée talked
to me about the child I felt all the more attracted to her. I think
somewhere inside that was the thought of my father who was
also not around when I was a kid. And together with it was the
fact that Clarence wanted to go out with Desirée, but I was the
one who actually did.

She turned up at the hotel next day with the little girl who was
very pretty, like her mother, and very quiet, and whom I liked
very much.

Desirée and I met every evening after that until I was due to
go back to sea. She would leave the child with her mother and
we would eat or go to a club and I would talk about ships. She
was my first girl friend in any real sense and I enjoyed the new
experience. I did the talking and she listened and it never occurred
to me to ask how she lived, or anything like that. At sea everything is provided for you and consequently you never even think
of the responsibilities of people on shore, like paying the rent,
buying food and all that.

The night before I was due to leave—on a week's trip to Fin-

land and back, to be followed by a three-month tour—we talked
about what we wanted to do with ourselves. I didn't want to do
anything, as I remember, except keep going to sea. And suddenly
Desirée was crying and didn't want me to go. This was an un-
heard of scene for me. Who cries about me going anywhere?
It drew me very close to her. For the first time, I thought, someone
cares something.

You don't hurt people who care. I wanted to do something
about it and I told her I would think about staying ashore when
the trip was over.

I went off to Finland and we wrote to each other and when
the ship returned to England she was at the docks at Sittingbourne on the Kent coast waiting for me. She said she would stay
with me until the ship left.

I found this a bit frightening. I was very eager for her friendship and a part of me wanted to get more deeply involved, but at
the same time I experienced nothing of the sense of excitement I
would feel now at the prospect of spending a weekend with an
attractive woman. Nowadays one can play games, talk, listen to
music, or just stay in bed. But in those days I couldn't think what
we would do.

However, I saw the Chief Officer and said Desirée was my
wife, which enabled me to get a pass for her to stay on board
while we were docked. As usual, I worked while we were in port
so as to make some extra money. Desirée stayed in my cabin during the day and when I'd finished working, in the evening, we
would eat together, either in the mess or in a local pub, before
going back to my cabin.

For some reason I was not very eager to go to bed with her
and when we did come around to it I remember having a lot of
doubts, which I tried to keep from her. My feeling for her hardly
embraced physical sex. It concerned, rather, being with another
human being and caring about her. I suffered quite a bit of torture about the sexual side, due to a lot of conflict in me. I had
missed the normal teenage scene of having girl friends, due to
being at sea, and with the few women I'd made it with before
there had been no big emotional upheaval. I think somewhere
deep inside me I wanted to create the romantic scene boys have
with their first girl friends : the starry-eyed thing of young people
in love, going out dancing and doing this and that. In fact, I
was working hard, painting and scraping the ship all day long and

then going straight into a little hick town. It seemed rather dread-
ful—and yet nice, too, in a different way.

In spite of my problems, Desirée was very kind and loving and
you can't lie in a tiny cabin bunk with someone who wants you
physically without eventually making it. After the first time I
never had any difficulty.

During the days we spent together, I was very happy and it
made me want what Desirée wanted—for me to come and live
with her in London when the trip was over. I said that I would
send money every month for her and the child and we agreed
that she should find somewhere for us to live.

By the time we sailed for Liverpool *en route* to the West Indies
I was very sad at parting from her. So sad, in fact, that when I
learned we were taking in British Guiana, where she came from,
I sent her a cable telling her to meet me in Liverpool if she could,
so that she could give me the address of her family and friends.
We spent another three days together in Liverpool and then I
set sail for the Caribbean.

From then on my feeling about things was different from any
previous experience. Most of the older sailors had wives and
when we came into port they would be buying presents to take
home. Now I began to do the same. I would thoroughly enjoy
myself choosing handbags, scarves, trinkets—anything that took
my fancy. And I began to wait for letters. And every island we
called at—Bermuda, the Bahamas, everywhere—I found myself
looking at the scene to see if Desirée and I could live there.

I did the same in Guiana, where I was fêted by her family. I
took two shipmates—an Irishman and a Swede—to meet them,
feeling as if I were taking them to my own home, and they fêted
them, too. They were neat and tidy people in every sense of the
word—West Indian middle class; the sort of people I had no
contempt for at that time.

So I looked at British Guiana wondering if we would go back
and live there, since it was now firmly established in my mind that
I would marry Desirée.

I never considered my own country, Trinidad, at all. That had
a lot to do with my mother. It was our next port of call and I
went ashore for the few hours we were there. It was three years
since I'd last seen my mother and she looked fifteen to twenty
years older. Usually I was pleased to see her for about the first
hour, but this time I wasn't pleased at all.

I had no great liking for her. There were too many hang-ups between us. For one thing, she had always supported her husband in scenes against me; for another, she'd always told me as a boy that she wasn't able to dress well because she had to spend the money on me. She'd made me feel terribly guilty about that. And yet when I sent her money she still wouldn't spend it on clothes. She squandered it on drink and went around looking awful. She would wear great, wide-brimmed straw hats which always upset me because they drooped around her head and made her look grotesque. Even my friends would say: 'Man, make her take off that terrible hat.' Once I lost my temper about the way she looked and I burned nearly all her clothes and gave her money to buy new ones. This was probably the wrong way to go about it; but no way seemed to be the right way. She still didn't buy clothes, just made do with those that escaped the bonfire.

She would make no constructive effort about anything. One time I returned home after she'd had a terrible fight with her husband who'd left her and I found she'd let the complete house and moved into a chicken shed in the back yard, which she claimed to have converted into a sitting room. That really upset me. I wanted my room when I came off the ship. Don't tell me she'd converted it. To me that was just a chicken house and always would be.

So this time I found things had got even worse. She'd had to sell the house because she couldn't keep up the mortgage payments—due to her drink bill—and she'd moved back to the wretched shack I'd first grown up in with my grandmother. I was very angry because I'd been sending her money regularly for years and her husband had made quite a bit with his taxi service and they'd had a nice new car every year—but now she'd lost the roof over her head.

She was spending up to two dollars a day on alcohol, a sum which would easily have paid off the mortgage. Her constant cry was: 'You don't know what I have to put up with.' I didn't want to know. I just couldn't take that scene with her. And I didn't want to live in Trinidad while she was around.

6

From the West Indies we sailed back to Europe, to Yugoslavia, and embarked on an escapade that had the press and Scotland Yard running around in circles.

We were discharging a cargo of bauxite at Rijeka and I went ashore to drink with some of my friends. It was my first visit to an Iron Curtain country and I'd absorbed all those stories about the hard life under Communism and felt very strongly about the lot of the poor people who lived there. These feelings were increased on arrival at the port when I noticed how much the longshoremen kept to themselves. In almost any port in the world I'd previously been to, I found the stevedores would sit around with the sailors during work breaks, drinking coffee, eating and smoking. But in Rijeka the Yugoslav dock workers went into little groups of their own and would not attempt to have any relations with the crew at all, except to do with the job. They were very generous. Sometimes I would go and deliberately join a group who were sitting around with their flasks and bottles of wine and all sorts of sausage with their bread. If I pointed to a piece of sausage and asked what it was, they would immediately offer it to me. They were very happy to give or share anything of their own. But when it came to taking something in return, that was a different story. I would see their eyes looking at a packet of cigarettes if I produced one, or glancing at my coffee, but if I offered them anything they would look at each other and then look away up the deck before saying no. I found it a rather distressing experience. Occasionally a Yugoslav would accept something from the crew and that would always appear to be when there were no dock guards around. I could only assume they were afraid.

I had never anywhere in the world seen the docks so full of guards. They would be patrolling the waterfront, posted on the ship's gangways scrutinising passes and faces, standing watching us from the dock gates. It was very easy to conjure in one's mind a picture of secret police and slave labour as encouraged by the Western press.

Once ashore, however, everything seemed much more normal, with people sitting under the striped umbrellas of the pavement cafés, laughing and drinking just as in other Mediterranean countries. At night, in the cheap, gay clubs of the dock area, there would be scores of people chattering and dancing Yugoslav dances. There was never any reluctance on the part of the attractive women who frequented these clubs to accept things from a foreigner.

It was in one of these clubs that my shipmates and I were getting rather drunk one night, talking to the local women, when they produced this attractive girl with the delightful name of Maria Salopec. She was dark with lovely long auburn hair. She spoke English with a charming, slightly American accent. And she was very anxious, for reasons we never discovered, to get out of the country. During our drunken conversation, somebody jokingly said why didn't we take her to England with us and she seized on the idea, pleading for all she was worth. Before we knew what was happening four of us were suddenly plotting like hell to get her onto the ship. This meant smuggling her past a Yugoslav policeman at the dock gates, another on the gangway of the ship and then our own night watchman. If we'd been at all sober we wouldn't have entertained the idea, but in our happy state at the time it seemed like the most exciting thing going. Preparing a plan of campaign at our table, voices drowned by the Yugoslav music, we made light of the difficulties—rightly so, as it turned out.

The five of us left the club together, the girl in the middle. We staggered up to the dock gates pretending to be more drunk than we were and two of us noisily surrounded the guard, blocking him in his hut, offering him cigarettes, slapping him on the back and generally making overwhelming nuisances of ourselves while

the other two smuggled the girl through. We got rid of the policeman on the gangway quite simply by one of us going on ahead
and offering him a cup of coffee if he cared to come below deck
to get it. He didn't hesitate. The night watchman was removed
from the danger zone by the simple expedient of my taking him
aside on the pretext of giving him detailed instructions about
morning calls while one of us quickly led the girl to an empty
cabin next to mine and settled her in.

Came the dawn and the full, hangoverish realisation of what we
had done, but the girl was now very eager to go on and the rest
of us felt obliged to finish what we had started.

It was a very tricky situation. For one thing, we had to prevent
the rest of the thirty or so crew from finding she was there. For
another, the ship was not heading straight back to England, but
was going on to Israel first to pick up a cargo of oranges. We
had to work out a detailed plan of operation with military pre-
cision to cover a long period.

We finally arranged that the girl should sleep during the day
and that at night we should take it in turns to get food to her
and smuggle her onto the deck where she could stretch her legs
and go to the toilet. In the meantime, one of us went ashore to
an address she gave us, with a note asking for her clothes. These
were wordlessly handed over in a brown paper parcel by another
girl. There were no questions from either side. We were probably
all a little too scared at what we'd got ourselves involved in.

Our operation was completely successful, however. Norwegian
boats are always lavish with their food and people were always
taking it out of the mess. We would simply fill an extra plate with
whatever was being served up—steaks, meat balls, fish, potatoes
—and take it down to the girl when nobody was around. The
only time there was any real danger was during the captain's
inspection of the ship. But I, as bosun, accompanied him and I
was able to steer him away from the cupboard where the girl
was hidden for the occasion.

Everything worked too well to last. We got back to London—
and disaster.

One of the reasons why things went wrong was that we got a
little lax. I was thinking about meeting Desirée and, doubtless,
the others were thinking about their wives and children. We didn't
pay the girl all the attention we should. We'd hidden her temporarily in the hatch with the Israeli oranges and the Customs

took us completely by surprise by coming aboard early. Of course, they found her.

The big interrogation started and the Special Branch of Scotland Yard was called in. The girl was terribly cool and refused to say how she got on board and who had helped her, but there was one Yugoslav in the crew and naturally everyone was convinced he had something to do with it. The combination of political implication and cheesecake was sniffed out in no time by the *Daily Mirror* and the newspaper carried a big story under the heading 'The Peach Among the Oranges'.

The preliminary investigations led nowhere and the authorities decided they would allow nobody off the ship—except that I was the one man with a British passport and they couldn't stop me. I went ashore, met Desirée, and we went to stay at her mother's house in North London.

While I was gone, it seems, the police searched the girl's handbag and found a photograph of me in it. I hadn't the slightest idea about this and I suppose she must have taken it from my cabin as a memento of the escapade. The result was that somebody phoned from Desirée's house that night and told her mother the police were looking for me. This was confirmed in next day's *Daily Mirror*.

I went back to the ship to avoid trouble and they put me through a long, fruitless interrogation. They tried a sneaky move, too, bringing the girl surreptitiously up behind me, so that she was right there when I turned, and then asking us both sharply if we knew each other. However, we were both convincing enough for them to let me go, but when I went to the purser for my wages, he told me they had been seized until everything was settled and, what was more, the captain had sacked me.

You can't argue with a sea captain, no matter how cavalier his treatment, so I left the ship without any money to find that Desirée's West Indian landlord had got terrified by the police visit, had given her notice and declared he wouldn't have me in the house under any conditions.

Desirée moved in with her mother and I took up an offer which had been open to me for some time from a West Indian who owned a drinking club in Notting Hill.

This was a club I had frequented during my numerous trips to England. Like most other sailors, I would feel lonely and, having plenty of money, would go into a club and drink a lot of rum

and invite other people to drink with me. It probably appeared
that I had a lot of capital and the West Indian who ran this particular club had long been asking me to go into business with him.
'All the boys like you,' he said. 'We would have the club filled
every night.' Once we had sat and talked, plying each other with
drink at the same time and it turned out that he wanted to open
another club and run one himself while I looked after the other.
I told him I was contracted for another trip and would talk about
it when I got back. So I got back and I was sacked, which settled
things. I went into the club and said: 'I've come. Let's get
started.'

The owner was delighted to see me—and all the Norwegian
sailors I always brought in with me—and he invited me to begin
work straight off. We never did get around to working out any
money business—but I was now half owner of a club.

In the meantime, the police put Maria Salopec under some
sort of cabin arrest while the Home Office decided what to do
with her. She told them she hadn't come for political asylum, but
because she loved a man. The photograph they'd found made me
the number one candidate. The next move was rather startling.
A couple of my fellow conspirators smuggled the girl off the ship
under the eyes of a Special Branch man. This may sound James
Bondish, but nobody knows a ship like the sailors who work on
it. If they decide to get somebody on or off, they will. What to
do with her once she was off was a different matter. For want of
any other ideas they brought her to the club, knowing that I
usually drank there. As it happened, I was out at the time, but
my new partner agreed, for the sheer devil of it, to hide the girl
and he had her taken to the house of a West Indian friend in
Willesden.

Now the hue and cry was really on. The *Daily Mirror* carried
a fresh headline, 'Peach Escapes', and when I next arrived at
the club a host of reporters descended on me saying, 'Where's the
girl?'

For the next three days those reporters and cameramen never
left the club. They settled in on a diet of double whiskies, keeping the story running, determined that I had all the answers they
wanted if they just stuck with me.

Drink sales in the club quadrupled. We sold out and had to
bring in another thirty cases of beer and whisky. The club was
booming and my partner, who left me in charge while he went off

gambling through the day, slapped me on the back and said: 'I knew you'd be great for business, man.'

That club lasted about three weeks, which was remarkable in the circumstances. It was running twenty-four hours a day with Fleet Street focusing on it in days when the authorities were hysterical about cellar clubs. The police made no move until long after everything had died down.

Three days later someone informed the police and they found the girl at the house in Willesden. It must have seemed a very obvious set-up to them. She had my photograph; she'd been taken to a West Indian club I was helping to run; she'd been removed to a West Indian house. And I was the only West Indian on the ship. They took me in for fresh questioning, but they knew I wasn't on the ship when she escaped and they couldn't pin anything on me.

Maria Salopec was taken into custody and shipped back to Yugoslavia where heaven knows what happened to her. Somebody in the Special Branch may still occasionally wonder what it was all about.

7

When black people start looking for somewhere to live in this country, there's only one sort of place where they don't have much difficulty and where there's no discrimination—the ghettoes.

You find the ghettoes in any city where there's a sizable black population. Nottingham has its 'Meadows', Manchester its 'North Side', Cardiff, 'The Bay'. And in London there are several: the Notting Hill area known as 'The Grove' after Ladbroke Grove; Brixton; the East End. They are the crumbling slums of the city, teeming with life above and below the surface, oppressively overcrowded, gripping their inhabitants in a claustrophobic tension. They produce a ghetto mentality and if you live in one of them the thinking of the place takes over your mind.

This thinking has a lot to do with the hustling that goes on when people are made to feel rejects, and with the paranoia that exists between the police and the residents. It's a very special community feeling—a feeling of working together, playing together, suffering together. The people inside the ghetto care about you. They'll help you out if you can't pay your rent, if you're broke, if the police want you. Anyone will hide you out. And in there you don't think in terms of who you'd like to have dinner with, but who would you go to if you were in trouble.

Living conditions in the ghettoes are terrible, though, and I wouldn't choose to live in them.

Desirée and I started looking everywhere else in London for

a home and we had the same dreary experience every other black person has : a desperate search through the *Evening Standard*, long treks to see places and immediate rejection when the landlord saw the colour of our skins. At least the advertisements on shop window notice boards were usually open about discrimination and saved us fruitless journeys.

After a few weeks of sheer frustration, we began to see there was really no alternative to the ghetto and eventually Desirée found a place for us in the Notting Hill area. It was a small room on the top floor of a house in S—— Street in the middle of one of the worst slums in London.

Together we went to see it . . . out of Westbourne Park Station, across the railway line and into Kensal Road, where it was impossible to believe you were in twentieth century England : terraced houses with shabby, crumbling stonework and the last traces of discoloured paint peeling from their doors, windows broken, garbage and dirt strewn all over the road, derelict cars . . . I remember thinking, 'We've done it now,' but when we turned into S—— Street it was even worse—every second house deserted, with doors nailed up and rusty, corrugated iron across the window spaces, a legion of filthy white children swarming everywhere and people lying drunk across the pavement so that we had to walk around them.

We came to the house which was to be our home and the African owner led us up the decrepit stairway to a room practically filled with ugly furniture and the noise of trains passing on the adjacent railway tracks. The floor was covered with worn linoleum, the single gas ring for cooking was outside on the dismal landing, there was no bath in the house—and he wanted £2 15s a week. We were desperate and we moved straight in.

By the time we'd installed a cot for the child and piled up our suitcases there was hardly room to turn around, but we were still better off than most others in the area. There can be several people living in the same room, sleeping in the same bed, and it's been that way since the nineteenth century. Records show the medical officer of health of more than a hundred years ago referring to a family of nine, the father ill with pleurisy, living in one dark room containing only a thousand cubic feet of air. That was one example amongst hundreds.

At night the ghetto takes on a different hue, a sexual quality. The daughters of all these families issue from their poky rooms all dressed up and start to ply their bodies for hire. They make a lot of money.

In the next room to ours lived a Trinidadian friend of mine named Nick, whose Italian girl friend also earned money by going out on the streets. It was the order of the day. Nobody was shocked by it. One way and another it was a hell of a place to bring up a child in.

The second day we were there I registered at the local Labour Exchange to try to get a job. I wanted work as a painter, which was one of the things I'd learned to do on board ship. It took me three minutes flat to find I wasn't going to get one. They told me straight out that there were jobs, but none for coloured people. It was the room scene all over again. No coloured for this, no coloured for that. After a number of rejections like that I wasn't looking very hard any more. I refused to hang around the Exchange all day, every day, the way some fellows did. When I chatted with Nick and told him of my experience, he laughed and said: 'Why you going there? You never get any work.' He'd seen the light the first time he ever went into the Labour Exchange.

Nick was a beautiful boy, tall and cat-like in his movements. He was a very happy person, who could find something to laugh at in almost anything that was said. Since he always had quite a lot of money, I suppose he could afford to laugh. He dressed very well and anywhere he wanted to go he took a taxi. That was quite impressive and, as I had nothing else to do with my time, I started going around with him to see what the other West Indians did.

During the day we would go to cellar clubs—quiet basements with a table, where people would gamble with dice or cards. Nick was quite serious about gambling and always knew just what he was doing. In the evening we would move on to the drinking clubs, which would be full of white and black hustlers playing the juke boxes and dancing with the smartly dressed prostitutes who came in for a breather. I began to get to know quite a lot of people and found myself spending more and more time in the clubs as a consequence. The fact is that even if you have a new woman and a child, a whole new scene, the idea of hanging around a tiny room with a cot and your suitcases and everything else isn't the most appealing in the world.

Sometimes in the clubs, Nick, who knew I had no money,

would give me a few pounds and tell me to shoot dice. I was never much of a gambler and invariably lost. I would stop playing, with some of the money still in my pocket and Nick would say, 'Keep it'. I would take it home and proudly present it to Desirée.

That was when I started hustling. I didn't realise it at the time, but that's how you drift into it. There's no money and people must eat and the rent must be paid. . . .

In the evenings a lot of prostitutes would come into the clubs loaded with money. There was one I used to talk to. I had no designs on her. It was just a relaxation. Prostitutes are pretty fascinating women if you can swing with them. If you meet them on the street for x pounds, that's something else, but on their own scene they're very earthy people with a lot of life and independence of character.

One evening, however, in a local club, she was crying and I asked her what the trouble was and she said her old man had just got nicked. One doesn't ask what for in those circumstances and I just made a few consoling noises. She asked me if I'd like a drink and I said I had no money. She took a £5 note from her purse and gave it to me. 'Go on—get us a drink,' she said.

By the time I returned with the drink, she already looked happier. I started to give her the change and she said: 'Keep it. I feel lucky tonight.'

After I got over my surprise, I was very happy to keep the change. We sat drinking and chatting and I looked at her a little more attentively than before. She was a typical pretty little English girl with rather sharp features and a good figure. She was twenty and looked seventeen. I suppose the most striking thing about her, apart from her beautiful clothes, was her short, black hair, which was streaked with silver in the style of the times.

We had another drink and then she said: 'I'm going out now. Will you be here when I come back?' I asked when that would be and she said it would be early. I told her I'd be there.

It may sound ludicrous today, but at that time I was quite green. I had no idea of being a ponce, nor yet of not being one. I hadn't thought about it at all. But there I was landed with four-pounds-something and a nice-looking lady saying would I be there when she got back. I told Nick and some of the other boys and they slapped me on the back and expected me to buy them drinks, saying, 'You're on,' as if I'd backed the Derby winner.

I was very happy and set off for home, picking up baby food and other provisions on the way. I gave Desirée a couple of pounds, which was very timely as we were flat broke, and I told her I was going out again to the gaming houses.

Around midnight I went back to the club and found the girl sitting there staring into her drink. Her face lit up when she saw me and she said: 'I thought you weren't coming.' We had a drink and then she said: 'Let's go.'

We went to her place which was a basement flat several blocks from the club. It looked dingy outside, but was luxurious inside— to me at any rate. To begin with there were fitted carpets throughout and then there was this exotic arch connecting a spacious front room with the bedroom. Admittedly the place was overfurnished with a lot of expensive things, like a massive record player, a liquor cabinet, pouffes, sofas. There was too much of everything, but for a man used to worn linoleum and suitcases, it was something to luxuriate in.

She offered me a drink, but I had coffee instead and we sparred with a bit of small talk while she put on a record. She asked me casually who my old lady was and for some reason I said I hadn't one. She asked where I lived and I said with my family, which was true enough. Did I know her old man, she wondered. He was a Jamaican and I'd seen him around. Then she began to talk about her night and how lucky she'd been. 'I picked up an old geezer and rolled him,' she told me.

At one point, while we chatted, she asked me: 'Why don't you sharpen yourself up?' I told her I'd only just arrived in England and didn't have money for clothes or anything else. Without a flicker of hesitation she picked up her handbag and produced her takings. I tried not to goggle at the sight of something over £40 and I watched while she separated a pound note and some small change and passed all the rest over to me. She said, almost apologetically: 'I must keep some for myself because I'm going to Brixton to see my old man tomorrow.'

People have been trying to work out why prostitutes need a ponce since the profession began and nobody's found a satisfactory answer. In this girl's case, I think she was a compulsive giver and she had no other way of making so much to give. The man could have been me or anyone else. I just happened to be there at the time, strange and new, when she found herself alone.

After the coffee and chit-chat, we both had a bath in a bathroom which seemed to me the most beautiful place in the world. In S—— Street there was no bathroom in the house and we had to fill a jug from a tap, heat the water in a kettle and pour it in a basin. I really luxuriated in that bathroom, which was sparkling and warm and full of sweet-smelling things. I could have stayed there all night even though the girl was waiting in bed.

I remember she had a beautifully formed body and she knew how to use it, which wasn't surprising. After all, it was earning a lot of money. It wasn't until the next day that I knew her name —Sylvia.

Although I wasn't rationalising at the time, I had entered into the relationship as a commercial proposition. It was nice that she was young and pretty, but it wouldn't really have mattered.

We slept late and ate a huge breakfast, which she obviously enjoyed preparing. When she started getting dressed about mid-day to go and visit her old man, I made some excuse that I had things to do and said I would meet her that evening at the club. She was afraid I might not turn up and made me promise to be there.

As I walked into number 22 S—— Street, I bumped into the landlord and proudly paid him two weeks' of arrears and a week's rent in advance.

Desirée started throwing a scene as soon as I appeared. Where had I been? What was I doing all night? I wouldn't tell her anything except to say I'd gone into the country with some of the boys to earn some money. I didn't want to talk about it. Forget it. I told her I'd paid the landlord, which cooled her down somewhat, and I gave her £10—which was like a million to us in those days. She began to be concerned about me. 'You must be tired,' she said, 'out working all night.' 'No, I'm not,' I said. 'Go and do some shopping.' I avoided going with her. I had to start taking precautions. I was in the jungle.

When I started to change my clothes I was very glad I'd sent Desirée out on her own : my skin was covered with silver paint from Sylvia's hair, which would have given the game away before it started. By the time she came back with a load of groceries and started to cook, I had thoroughly cleaned myself up.

Desirée started questioning me again about how I'd got the money and I had to put on a big James Bond act. I said I would be having money from now on, but it was a tricky situation and

I'd tell her about it when it was all worked out. I felt a little guilty about that, but my worst moment was to come. For a man who'd been out working all night, I was remarkably unhungry. I nearly choked getting Desirée's food down while she stood solicitously over me. Later that day I went into the gaming houses with £15 of the £20 I had left and gambled every penny away. I think I wanted to show everyone that I had money at last.

That night Desirée wanted to know if I would be in later. I said I didn't know and she wasn't very happy about that. I could see the problems coming up and I spoke to Nick about it, asking his advice about what story I should give her. Nick began by saying : 'That's a good thing—don't let it get away.' By *it* he meant Sylvia. She was not a woman; she was a business enterprise. And then he gave me his advice, which was simple, but effective. I should explain to Sylvia that I couldn't sleep at her place since it was her gaff—where she did her work—and I would probably get busted if I hung around there. 'That way you can leave early,' Nick said. 'But to keep her interested, say you're looking for somewhere else to live.'

At midnight I was in the club waiting for Sylvia to show up. The hours went by and I'd spent the remaining money on drinks and began to feel quite miserable. I thought I wasn't going to see her any more and by that time I was quite hooked on the idea of being rich. I had no moral feelings about it. Everyone in the area was selling something. It was all the same to me.

Anyway, she did turn up eventually and wanted to leave immediately, as she was tired. We went back to her place to bed and she told me things had been a bit rough so she hadn't earned all that much. It came to a clear £22, however, which didn't seem to me to be much to complain about. She gave me £20 and kept the odd £2 for herself.

While we were in bed I gave her the spiel that Nick had suggested and she got suddenly sentimental and didn't want to see me get busted. This was fine as it meant I was able to leave her place in the small hours and hotfoot it back to S—— Street, where I undressed and got into bed forgetting all about the silver paint.

In the morning I was roused by a hell of a scene going on. Desirée was screaming her head off. 'You got a woman! You got a woman!' I began denying it like crazy. 'Where does that money come from?' she yelled. 'There's something happening.' I said. 'You bet there's something happening,' she screamed. 'A woman with silver hair's what's happening!' 'You mustn't listen to people telling you these things . . . this gossip,' I said. 'Gossip!' She was beside herself. 'I suppose that's gossip all over your skin!'

And there I was like an Indian in war paint.

I didn't know what to say. What was there to say? So I told her : 'This lady offered me some money and I took it.' 'It can't go on!' Desirée cried. 'It's better if you go back to sea!' I said I didn't want to go back to sea and Desirée demanded to know if I intended going on with this girl. I said I didn't intend to sleep with her, but if I could raise money for us I'd carry on raising it. Desirée said not with her, I wouldn't. I could take my money and pack up. I tried sweet reason. I pointed out that we had a child and that none of us had any money before, but now we had. The rent was paid. There was food in the house. Prospects. . . . Desirée said it would carry on over her dead body. 'All right,' I said. 'I'll just have to go straight out and look for something else to do.' 'You're going with your woman,' Desirée accused. 'No I'm not,' I said. 'I'm going to find some other way to make money.' And I left, thankful to get out of there.

I went straight to Sylvia's house and let myself in with a key she'd given me. That just shows how naïve I was. Sylvia was in bed with this little, fat, old English guy and there I am walking straight in as if I'm coming home. The guy jumped out of bed, his ardour all rampant still, and stared at me in fright. Sylvia was staring at me more in sorrow than in anger. Everyone was staring at me. I felt acutely embarrassed and said something like, 'I'm very sorry.'

I walked back out and went to a basement club nearby where I sat not knowing whether to laugh or be penitent. I'd just had no idea of Sylvia's timetable for hustling.

Very shortly afterwards a fellow came down and said someone wanted to see me upstairs. I went up to face Sylvia.

'Why did you do it?' she asked.

I said quite truthfully that I'd no idea she'd have anyone there and she looked in my face and saw that I meant it. We went back to her house to eat something and she started telling me about her schedules—how she started work as soon as she'd finished visiting her old man and that I should keep clear of the flat from that time on. She said the little old guy was a good, regular client of hers and she'd nearly lost him because my sudden appearance had terrified him. I promised I wouldn't do it again. Nick nearly burst at the seams laughing when I told him the story.

I continued to see Sylvia, returning to S—— Street at three or four in the morning having carefully removed all traces of silver paint. I told Desirée I was gambling. I don't think she really believed it, but she wanted to very much and the daily sums I gave her—anything from £7 to £15—no doubt helped her to convince herself. Every day I had a minimum of £20. I didn't save any, but I had some good suits made. I spent the rest on gambling in the clubs during the afternoons.

The Jamaican Sylvia had been living with had so many previous convictions that he was committed to quarter sessions and kept in custody. He and the girl had some kind of argument during visiting hours and she suddenly stopped going to see him. As a result of this I had a visit from two of his Jamaican cronies one day to warn me to lay off his girl. They came into a club where I was gambling with some Trinidadian friends and started menacing me. There was a rather bitter inter-island rivalry among West Indians for the ladies of Notting Hill. But these Jamaicans had made the mistake of meeting me on my home ground and the Trinidadians told me: 'Tell them to fuck off.' And that's just what I did. They didn't stay to argue the point. They must have figured that was the wrong place to try anything. When I met Sylvia later I learned they'd been to see her, too, and got equally short shrift. She told them if they messed around she'd see them in gaol.

Around this time Sylvia became more insistent that I should find us somewhere to live together. I hadn't really been looking, but then she put me on the spot by giving me an address where she knew there was a flat vacant.

I went to see it in Westbourne Park Road. I was dressed very sharp, with shining shoes and two rings on my finger like any other ponce in the area, and the African landlord was clearly very keen for me to take it. With my back smack against the wall I had sudden inspiration. I asked him if it would be all right for my old lady to work there and said I'd give him extra money. He said certainly not, his was a respectable house. And that was the end of that.

From then on I became very professional about the whole affair with Sylvia. I began to realise that ladies come and go and that they were always available in the area. When Sylvia pushed the idea of a flat, I'd tell her: 'To hell with it—let's pack it up.' I didn't care if she came or went, except from a business point of view and she was forced to accept it

The flat I did take, finally, was for Desirée and the child, not for Sylvia. It was in St Stephen's Gardens and was magnificent by S—— Street standards. It had a big room, with a smaller one at the side for a kitchen. There was a toilet on the landing outside and a communal bath two flights away. The rent was £6 10s, which was nothing in my new-found state of affluence. Desirée was delighted with it, even though she must have had deep-seated anxieties about where the money was coming from.

Somebody once told Sylvia something and, for the first time, she said: 'I hear you have a black wife.' I said, with truth, that I didn't have a wife and she didn't press the issue. She went on working like a maniac. She just loved to get up and go out on the streets. The only other thing she ever showed the least interest in was my buying new clothes. She would even bug me about that. We never talked about money any more. There was a box beside her bed where she put the notes and I just took them out. Whenever Nick and I discussed her, he would say how great it was and that his woman never brought in more than £10 because she was lazy.

We gambled a lot and he always won and I hardly ever did except once when I cleared £150—which nowhere near equalled my overall losses. I gave Sylvia £50, tickled to give her money for a change, and she asked me: 'What shall I do with it?' She was quite at a loss. I never gave her money again.

The end came about four months after I'd first met her. I had begun to frequent a new club which was more intimate and sophisticated than my normal haunts. It had soft music in place of the juke box and the people were well dressed. Sylvia and I drank there occasionally and thought it very cool. Then one day the African owner gave a cocktail party for some Nigerian diplomats and invited me. It was a big production and I thought it would be nice for Desirée to go, so we got her mother down to look after the child and went off to enjoy ourselves. We hadn't been there ten minutes when Sylvia walked in. Desirée took one look at her with her silver hair and knew immediately who she was. It was terribly embarrassing. I said to Desirée: 'Let's go,' and she said: 'I'm not going—I'm enjoying myself.' I told her

I had to go and have a word with Sylvia and she said: 'Is that the woman who's been giving you all that money?' I said: 'Please don't make a scene here. Just cool it.'

I went over to Sylvia and asked her if she wanted a drink. She said: 'Why don't you take me to your table with your friends?' I said it would be too embarrassing and she said: 'Is that your wife?' I told her: 'It's the woman you once asked me about.' 'Don't worry,' Sylvia said. 'I'll go.' I said she didn't need to do that, but I didn't try to stop her and I was relieved when she took off.

I went back to Desirée and she was having one of those unpredictable feminine reactions, laughing and treating it as a big joke. 'You're going to lose your woman now,' she said.

She was right. I tried to contact Sylvia later that same night, but I couldn't find her anywhere and somebody told me in a club that she'd gone off with Joey, an old friend of mine from Trinidad. I knew then what was happening: I was being exchanged on the market.

I saw her next day and said I wanted to talk to her and she told me there was nothing to say. I didn't argue. I said: 'Well—swinging.' I saw Joey, too, and he said: 'That's life, boy. Better me than someone else; I'm your friend.' I thought that was true enough. It was the sort of scene that happened to every ponce at some time or another.

It seems that during the period of dual existence, I acquired the reputation of being something of a hard man among the hustlers of Notting Hill. The way they saw it was that I sent this girl out to work and allowed her to do nothing but stay on the job constantly. In fact, of course, she seemed to want to do nothing else.

As far as I was concerned she was simply a business and it so happened that she was pretty, which made her amusing to walk around with occasionally—and she was nice to go to bed with. But I developed no personal attachment to her and I suppose I hurt her pride by bringing my woman to the party instead of keeping her in the background.

I still see Sylvia now and again in passing. She's still hustling like mad. It's her scene.

8

Whatever money I ever had was in my pocket and now that Sylvia had moved on I had no income and the problem of bills to pay. Or rather Desirée had the problem of bills to pay because one never has these things at sea and I had still to come to terms with them. When I brought her money, it was not really because I recognised the responsibility I had to pay the bills; it was simply that I wanted to give her something.

So now I would prowl around the area every day from one gaming house to another, gambling for small stakes on the dice games and searching for some way to make more money.

It was at this time that I embarked on what to my mind was my first criminal undertaking. Inside the gaming houses you find all manner of misfits: ponces, pickpockets, small-time crooks. They sit around discussing their sexual conquests, sometimes arguing religion or politics, but, above all, planning criminal activities which, in their sheer desperation, they hope will make them a fortune overnight. It was in this setting that I got word somebody wanted to talk to me about a job. Even though this was not my normal field of activity, I could hardly say no. I'd gained a reputation in the ghetto for being a very wide-awake fellow.

I was taken to a room not far from my favourite gaming house to meet two Barbadians I'd seen around in the clubs. One of them, called The General, marked the games played in some of the houses. He was a quiet, retiring guy who wore spectacles and always looked the height of respectability. The other one, Jake, ran an illicit taxi service in the area.

They put their cards straight on the table: they wanted to stick up a post office in Reading. They had street plans laid out ready, and lists of times and movements.

Talking about this sort of robbery in the ghetto is like discussing the weather. It goes on all the time, for want of anything better to do, helping to feed the poor man's fantasies of wealth. I wasn't at all shocked or surprised. I just sat and listened.

It seemed that the General had been casing the joint one day a week for some weeks. On this particular day, at a certain time, there was only one employee in the office and something like £7,000 in the till. It was a very easy job, he said. Nobody would be harmed. We would just go in, overpower the guy behind the counter and take the money—which would be more than £2,000 each. They convinced me they were professional gentlemen at this sort of thing and I agreed to go in with them. It did come out in conversation that Jake had been on a number of jobs before as a driver, but it's not usual to query anyone's credentials.

We went to Reading on a trial run and every detail was exactly as they had forecast. I went in and bought a postal order to check that there was only one employee in charge and saw the fat wads of notes in a drawer. Like they said, it would be easy.

A week later we went down for the job. Jake drove the car, as planned, to a car park outside Reading, where he swapped it for another and came on to the town in the stolen vehicle to meet us. It was his job to sit in the car across the street with the engine running while the General and I went into the post office. The General would approach the long counter, stick his gun in the employee's ribs and hustle him into a back room while I scooped the money into a bag. If everything went well, we would tie the fellow up, close the doors and leave.

I had gone into the job from sheer frustration, but at the moment of action I felt quite excited, with a sense that I was moving into the big time.

The General and I walked into the post office and it was empty just as it should have been. And then the General fainted. Passed clean out on the threshold.

To say I was nonplussed is an understatement. For a second or two my mind went completely blank and I stared from the horizontal General to the goggle-eyed clerk behind the counter. Then I figured I couldn't very well leave the General there, so I picked him up and carried him out to the car, watched all the way by the astonished clerk who didn't move or say a word. Jake drove like hell away from that post office and by the time we reached the car park and transferred to his own car, the General was only just coming round. Jake and I were beginning, by then, to see the funny side of it and Jake was saying we should have shot the General and left him there and the General was saying: 'What happened? What happened?'

'Michael shot the man and you passed out,' Jake said. And the General promptly passed out again on the back seat.

We got him to his flat in London and for days he shut himself up inside, merely poking his head through a window twice a day to ask a friend to buy all the newspapers. We played it straight and he never knew the truth until days later. After that, of course, nobody would ever go on a job with him again. The story's still one of the favourite jokes in the gaming houses of Notting Hill: the General shut up in his house.

That was the first and last robbery of this type I attempted, though Jake and I came out of it with enhanced reputations. We were considered very cool operators not to have lost our heads. People would look at us in the clubs, imagining we were involved in all sorts of big crime. But in fact, all I was doing for some time was organising games, marking up score cards and gambling a little myself.

Life with Desirée was much better now because she knew I wasn't involved with another woman. She wanted me to find a respectable job, even if it meant going back to sea. But a part of me liked the landlubber's existence in spite of the frustrations and tensions, and I had no desire to go back on board ship. I figured that Desirée had a little saved and I made enough for us to get by on. The child had food and clothing and didn't appear to want for anything. Looking back, of course, I see that a child needs very much more than just money coming into the house, but I had no time to give her. My only thought every day had to be directed at how to find some money, how to go out and graft. It didn't leave room for anything else.

Eventually, with my now established reputation, I was invited by some other Trinidadians to help plan a robbery. It was to be from an estate agent in the area. They knew he collected thousands of pounds every week. That was the first time I heard the name, Peter Rachman.

These boys said he owned all the property in the area and I

found this included the house I lived in. Every Friday, they said,
he had all this money in his office, but the big problem was the
three big Alsatians he always had there too.

I decided I would take a look at the place and I went to the
office in Monmouth Road. It was in a basement, with entry by
a steep flight of stone steps. Rachman was sitting at his desk when
I went in and the dogs were sprawled around the room. There
were also two men who looked like bodyguards, one just sitting,
the other reading a newspaper. Rachman was a good-looking
man with a strong face and a balding head. He was very well
dressed and groomed and spoke in a quiet voice which I never
heard him raise. In short, he exuded quiet charm. He asked what
he could do for me and I said I lived in one of his houses and
would like somewhere better than my present flat. He asked what
was wrong with it and I told him I would prefer a self-contained
place with my own bathroom. He took my name and said he
would bear me in mind if anything came up—and that was the
end of our first meeting.

I told the Trinidadians that I couldn't see any answer to the
problem of the dogs and I left them talking about it, talking, talking. . . . Talk of this sort goes on all the time in any ghetto and
nine tenths of it never graduates to activity. These Trinidadians
all had ladies on the streets earning them money and this talk
was just a time-filler. Anyway, the robbery never came off.

Rachman did bear me in mind and some time later he put me
on to a flat in Powis Square which he was having redecorated.
It was a basement flat with a small front room, a very large back
room and a nice bathroom and kitchen. It was £8 a week and I
snapped it up. Desirée was delighted. The flat was not all that
beautiful, but for people who had lived in one room with a gas
ring, no bathroom and the toilet several stair flights away, it was
like a dream. It was, in fact, not bad as slum houses go. Structur-
ally it was pretty sound, just needed fresh paint and paper.

Desirée was particularly knocked out by the bathroom. She
liked to bathe twice a day, which is fairly customary in the West
Indies as it's so hot. She stayed in the bathroom for a long time
turning the water on and off and feeling the hot water as it ran
into the bath. And then she moved to the kitchen, which was a
real one, not a makeshift conversion, and she ran her hands along
the shelves and tried the taps on the gas stove. And then on to
the sitting room and the bedroom and she began delightedly

working out how we would paint this a certain colour and that another and put such-and-such here and something else there.

As soon as we actually moved in, three art students—an Australian, an Englishman and a Dutchman—came down from the floor above and introduced themselves, asking if there was anything they could do for us. They sat and chatted and we made them tea, which was a very nice neighbourly scene we were quite unused to. In the following weeks, they had parties with a lot of young friends from St Martin's Art School and they would invite us. In this new atmosphere Desirée bloomed as a woman. I saw her cooking for people and creating dishes I had no idea she knew how to make. We started actually enjoying life as human beings.

There were lots of new experiences for us. It was the first time we had lived in a house in England where we didn't have to push money into a gas meter, but paid quarterly bills instead. And we had our first telephone installed, which revealed to me how powerful an instrument it was in communication, how one could accomplish so much more—particularly helping people when they were in trouble and needing doctors, lawyers and things like that.

Although there was a lot of new-found happiness, there were drawbacks, of course. Outside there were brothels all the way down the street and opposite was the Blues Club which blasted on into the small hours. Adjacent Powis Terrace was immensely overcrowded with coloured families who spent a lot of time in the street and at night there were lots of fights and a great amount of police activity. If you stepped outside your door it was like being in Piccadilly Circus on a day when something riotous was happening there.

There were hang-ups inside, too, due to the vast Irish family living on the top floor. They were really more like a colony: something like eighteen children and ten adults living in four rooms. I never could succeed in counting them all as they came and went about their business. They were rather dirty people, which was inevitable with the overcrowding, and they made their bare living, appropriately enough, by dealing in junk. Most of this was stored in the ground floor passage as there was no room in the flat. To enter the house was like stepping into one great scrap heap. You had to claw your way over bicycle wheels, saucepans, rusty springs, broken-down prams, battered bedsteads . . .

anything metal you could name and quite a lot that was un-
nameable. Their *pièce de résistance*, spirited in one night to con-
front the tenants in the morning, was an entire railway wagon.
This might have caused some trouble in the household since it
blocked the entrance hall completely, but fortunately it got
jammed and the police came and removed it next day.

I very quickly got into the habit of using the basement area
entrance to my flat rather than face the ever-changing hazards
presented on the ground floor.

Having the flat created a whole new scene for us. Lots of people
would come in and sit talking with us, enjoying the comparative
comfort; people like my old school friend, Wilfrid Woodley, the
jazz pianist. Wilfrid, who has played in groups all over the country and on the Continent, is just about the finest piano player I
know, but he was having trouble finding somewhere to rehearse
so I invited him to install his piano in the sitting room.

Once Woodley started playing there, the word got around,
and lots of people started dropping in to listen to the jam sessions
he had with other instrumentalists, or to Desirée singing with him,
which she sometimes liked to do. Woodley took his rehearsals
very seriously, fanatically even, demanding that everyone arrive
on time and that every piece be played over and over again until
it was exactly right. I've known him to get angry with another
player's performance and take his instrument away to demon-
strate how he wanted a phrase done. There were some great performances nonetheless and everyone in the area loved these shows
so much that eventually we began pooling a little money and
cooking a big pot of food for the gathering—usually peas and
rice with salted meat mixed up in it, West Indian style.

Woodley had some trouble keeping a group together because
he was a real perfectionist and wanted to keep his boys at rehearsals all the time. But they needed money, just to live on, and en-
gagements were very scarce at the time. That was why we decided
to throw our first blues dance.

This sort of social gathering is a regular happening with West
Indians in an area like Notting Hill. The ghetto had no social
amenities, no community hall, no public place where a band
could play to people and amuse them, so it had to be done in
private flats. Since West Indians are basically a drinking people
and want a scene where they can sit and drink as well as dance,
there has to be a bar and this makes the whole thing illegal. Nor-

mally, this type of dance was run by men calling themselves
Duke this and Count that, who had big collections of records
which they would play with a system of microphones. They would
have the latest discs from America and the West Indies and
people would come from far around to listen.

Ours was different from these in that we had live music. We
had Woodley, a drummer, a bass player and a saxophonist and
our aims were to enable them to rehearse and get paid for it and
to make some money ourselves.

Blues dances are not very complicated to organise. We simply
cleared the floor, put a table across the kitchen door to serve as a
counter and stocked up with a whole load of canned beer. We
charged 2s 6d to come in and 2s 6d for each beer—and we just
didn't have enough room to accommodate the rush. The first
dance we held made between £60 and £70 profit, split fifty-fifty
between Woodley and his group and Desirée and me.

We began to throw these dances regularly and they were
enormously popular. There was just one snag. Once the music
really got under way, people stopped dancing and started crowding around the orchestra just to listen, the fellow at the door left
it unguarded to dig the music close up and the barman deserted
his bar. Woodley was a sort of Pied Piper of jazz. Everyone
dropped everything and became a doting audience.

We put up the entrance fee to 5s as a guarantee for the band
since the bar, our main source of income, just couldn't compete
with the music for popularity. We were working on how to deal
with this problem when a bigger scene evolved which needed all
our energies.

We began to hear the first tales of black people being beaten
up in the area, by whites.

9

The thing about the so-called Notting Hill race riots is that they were not real race riots at all.

People are always fighting in an area like the ghetto; clubs are always being invaded and broken up. And this was mid-summer (August 1958), the time of year when violence is always nearest the surface, particularly in poor, overcrowded areas.

The first night I heard these stories of beatings-up, I was in a club and I went out into the streets to see what was happening. But nothing was.

The next day the newspapers were full of the 'race riots' in Nottingham and I remember putting on my old seaman's clothes to be ready for anything and going out to see if these 'riots' had arrived in London. I toured the clubs and visited friends in their rooms, but nobody seemed to be getting worked up and the general opinion was that a few Teddy Boys had simply been making a nuisance of themselves.

That night a petrol bomb was thrown into one of the clubs, a West Indian got shot in the leg and there were odd bits of fighting here and there. But it was very far from being a race riot. Until the newspapers gave the term headlines again the following morning and shot up the temperature.

Throughout the day police cars were constantly cruising around the area and West Indians were meeting in clubs, or on street corners, to talk about what was supposed to be happening. I was one of them and at one point I was talking to some English friends who lived nearby when a police car pulled up across the street and a police officer got out and came over to us. He looked at me and said : 'You—off the streets!'

I ignored him. There were five of us chatting and he hadn't paid any attention to the others. He poked me then and repeated : 'You—get off the streets!' I said : 'What do you mean—me or us?' He replied : 'I'll give you two minutes to get off the streets.'

It didn't make any sense to me. I continued to ignore him and went on talking with my friends.

'All right,' he said and he crossed the street and drove off.

Three minutes later a car came screeching up and three policemen burst out and bundled me inside.

They took me to the nearby police station where the charge room was a very strange sight. One side of the room was full of West Indians looking bewildered. On the other side were three or four white guys. And in the middle were a line of policemen and a police sergeant sitting at a desk covered with broken bottles, knives, pieces of iron, razors. . . .

I joined the West Indian side and we waited in silence for some twenty minutes. It was quite a mystery. There was no riot —and yet there we were inside.

Then the ritual began with the West Indians. A young policeman took the first man to the desk and the sergeant said : 'What's he charged with?' The policeman picked up a piece of iron off the desk and replied : 'Armed with this weapon to commit a felony.' The sergeant took the iron, put a tag on it and sent the West Indian off for fingerprinting as a prelude to a night in the cells. 'Next!' the sergeant called and the performance was repeated with the next in line.

At one point one of the West Indians said : 'That's not mine, sir, I'm not signing for that.'

The sergeant looked him up and down and said : 'You're one of those, are you? All right—take him upstairs.'

Two policemen grabbed him on either side and took him away.

All this had a very funny effect on me. By the time I reached the desk I was crying, not from fear or concern for myself, but because the whole scene was so terribly sad. Before the sergeant could speak, I said : 'Which one is mine?'

He started to laugh and perhaps he felt a little sorry for me, because he said jokingly : 'No. We have something else for you.' The sergeant asked my policeman : 'What did this one do?' The

officer said I was on the streets and he gave me a repeated warning to move and I wouldn't. The sergeant charged me with obstructing the police in the execution of their duty and I was duly
fingerprinted and sent down to the cells.

There were fourteen West Indians in my cell, eleven charged
with being armed to commit a felony and three with obstructing
the police in the execution of their duty. One man spent the
whole night crying because he couldn't get over how it happened
to him. He was on his way home from work and the police were
picking up people in the street. He stopped to see what it was all
about and they arrested him. He cried throughout the night, sitting on the concrete floor of the cell and I sat near him unable
to sleep for thinking about the total lack of human dignity in
the whole scene.

Apart from the mental stress, it was not the most comfortable
night I'd ever spent. The cells were really designed for two and,
even with the narrow wall bench draped with snoring figures,
there was still hardly room for the rest of us to huddle on the
cold floor. I remember there was a toilet pail at one end of a
bench and in the morning someone got up to urinate and the
sudden hollow din served as reveille.

They let us out two at a time to wash and have breakfast. Our
numbers had increased since my arrival the previous night, but
there was no race war in the station. No animosity at all. Little
conversations sprang up between blacks and whites: 'What did
they put on you?' . . . 'Give us a fag mate—I don't want to ask
those bastards' . . . 'How's your lumbago?'

We were taken to Bow Street locked in tiny compartments in
a black maria. I spent the time constructing what I was going
to tell the magistrate.

The public gallery of the court was full of people from the
ghetto who had come to see what happened to their friends. Most
prisoners were remanded in custody straight off. The rest of us
were kept waiting till the end of the list.

When it came to my turn, I listened indignantly to the evidence
which described how the police tried to clear everyone off the
footpath and I'd refused to move so they had been forced to
arrest me. The impression I got was that the street had been full
of thugs with flick knives and that violence had been on the point
of erupting. I had pleaded not guilty and I gave my version of
the incident. The magistrate hardly gave me time to get the last

word out before he said : 'I find you guilty. The fine will be three
pounds with two guineas costs, or an alternative of fourteen days
in prison. Do you want time to pay?'

I felt pretty sick and I said : 'I'm not paying any fine. I'll
do the fourteen days.'

I was taken down to the cells, but within an hour, to my annoy-
ance at the time, some friend had paid my fine and I was released.

Back in Notting Hill everyone was talking about the so-called
riots and how they'd gone to court with bail for their friends
and no bail had been allowed. When I told people about the
police station scene they shook their heads with comments like :
'God, aren't they wicked—eh?'

That night I heard that a meeting was being held in a cellar
club called the Calypso to discuss the situation. The situation, as
far as I could see, was being created by newspaper sensationalism
and police hysteria. Together they were having quite an effect.
There was no doubt by now that a 'situation' did exist.

I went along to the meeting which was packed with black
people. There were three West Indians on the platform, one of
whom did all the talking. He had a nice accent, a fine command
of words and he spoke with authority.

'What we have to do is form ourselves into committees,' he
said. 'We must elect officers and make representations to the
Police Commissioner and our M.P.'s.'

Accent, words, authority and a lot of shit in my view. I had
just landed in court through police action and here he was saying we should go to the police for redress. I stood up and asked
leave to speak. Everybody looked at me and I said : 'You don't
want committees and representations. What you need is to get a
few pieces of iron and a bit of organisation so that tonight when
they come in here we can defend ourselves.'

My first public speech was very short and simple. Nobody
could say the message was obscure. And nobody could deny the
result was electrifying. There was an uproar of supporting cries.
I'd told them all just what they wanted to hear.

I don't think anybody was too clear about who the enemy was :
the police, white people, anyone who'd raise a hand against us.
We began preparing for whoever it might be. People were standing around discussing strategy; others were bringing in all sorts
of implements for weapons; a few American servicemen were demonstrating how to make petrol bombs. It was a sad scene, but

inevitable. We were finally standing up for ourselves against a hostile white world.

From then on we had a full military operation going, sallying out in small groups while the women in the club made coffee and sandwiches. Many of these women were white ladies living with West Indians, which gave the racial side an odd twist. They didn't think about whom they were fighting; they were simply supporting their men.

Throughout the night the violence in Notting Hill was as haphazard as it had been before and even accidental. We made only two planned attacks on a large scale. One was against a building used by a fascist group, the other against a club used exclusively by whites who were considered hostile to us. As reports came in that white men were seen entering these places in large numbers, we decided attack was the best form of defence. We split up and some of us lobbed petrol bombs in the back of the buildings while the rest waited in ambush out front. When they ran out into the street, the whites were dealt with sufficiently well to ensure they were out of the combat for the night.

But these incidents were exceptional. In general, people just drifted into violence, finding themselves involved without knowing how or why. The press was screaming that there were race riots, so people just couldn't keep away. The irresponsible journalism which exaggerated a few isolated incidents into large-scale racial disturbances brought sightseers into the area in their thousands. The sensible thing to do would be to stay away, but there's always a large section of any population which is attracted to riots for kicks and to relieve the boredom of dull lives. With a few wild ones throwing bottles, everyone tends to get involved. And white people don't run to the blacks for protection, nor the blacks to the whites. They separate into their own colour groups. And then you have it, created out of nothing—a race riot. Or at least, the atmosphere of a race riot. In actual fact, there still wasn't much real action. We had plenty of men coming back to the club to be with the ladies, the coffee and the sandwiches, and telling fantastic tales of how they'd just escaped this or that mob by the skin of their teeth. But we had only one casualty—a guy with his head cut open. He got the attention of a returned war hero.

The ghetto was swarming with policemen, too, all of them very hostile to the blacks. And they figured in the scene which, for me, symbolised the unreal, farcical quality of the whole affair.

We got a message in the club that one of our men, a Trinidadian named Clydie, was being attacked and outnumbered a couple of blocks away. We rushed reinforcements to the scene just in time to see Clydie and half a dozen of the rest of the boys being herded into the back of a police van. At the moment we arrived, someone threw a petrol bomb at the black maria and it exploded near the driver. He leapt out in alarm, leaving the front empty, and as the police pushed everyone in at the back so they went straight through and out the front like some old Laurel and Hardy film, to the accompaniment of cheering, clapping and laughter from the huge mixed audience of white and black.

I remember the next day the newspapers went to town with headlines like: 'Most violent eruptions yet seen' and all that, but the disturbance had already played itself out by that time.

10

The aftermath of the riots was one of deep shame inside the area. Amongst the legion of hustlers no colour is recognised. Specialists work together and have no colour, whether their line is sex, housebreaking, bank robbery or pick-pocketing. And now there was a lot of embarrassment about what each individual had been doing over the previous few days.

The white criminals would filter back into the black clubs, saying: 'It wasn't us man. All those people came from outside.'

This was true to some extent, as the charge sheets of those arrested showed. An enormous number of addresses were outside the area. But deep down, we felt that everyone had been involved. It was just that the whites in the ghetto knew better how to evade the police. Not that we admitted this consciously. We were very eager to accept any excuse to prove that our fellow misfits had not ganged up with the other whites against us.

As a result of the trouble, Notting Hill gained official recognition as a problem area and sociologists, professional and amateur, began to flood the area, together with their cohorts of students, titled ladies and do-gooding young middle-aged women. They literally came in droves—all of them terribly well-intentioned, quite clueless and full of questions. They all wanted to do something for the poor, unfortunate residents of Notting Hill and they were desperate to meet us. You can't imagine how desperate some of those women were. I have never in my life seen so many ladies so hot in such a small space. They were so frustrated that I feel in some cases their deepest motive for coming into the area was sheer sexual need. Anyway, it was a field day for the black men, who had never realised social work could be so pleasurable. Some of them even set up permanent liaisons and are right now adding to the half caste population of this country.

One research group made a greater impact than any other. It was run by the sociologist Richard Hauser, and his wife Hepzibah, the concert pianist sister of Yehudi Menuhin. They had a large staff and were determined to organise us and help us to sort out our own problems, as they put it.

Since I was well known in the area, Mr and Mrs Hauser visited me and asked me to help in organising their first meetings. They wanted to get to know the people, they said, and to create group leaders in the community so that we could solve our ills once and for all. I listened to what I considered a lot of nonsense, but, mainly because Mrs Hauser was a woman of great charm and made me feel they meant what they said, I agreed to help.

I turned out a lot of people for the meetings, which were held in a local school. They were intrigued to see what this 'Institute of Group and Social Development' was all about. Mr Hauser spoke about brotherhood and described how he'd done similar community development work in Australia. He said he wanted a house-to-house canvas of the area, that he would train us in the techniques of interviewing people and that with the resultant information, methods of tackling the problems of Notting Hill would suggest themselves. Accommodation could be improved, the area cleaned up, prostitutes cleared off the streets and the brothels closed.

One of the many young white students in the audience said he didn't see how the problems would be solved unless the prostitutes and misfits were brought into the meetings. That hadn't really been Mr Hauser's idea and he was a little aghast.

'Am I to understand you want to bring pimps and prostitutes in here?' he demanded.

There was a great, resounding, 'Yes!' from the audience and the meeting had suddenly broken down in complete disorder.

That was the major difficulty for the do-gooders: really getting to know the people in the ghetto, where a large part of the population was so remote from anything they'd previously experienced.

In one noble attempt to get below the surface, the Hausers

asked me to organise a party for local people, which they would finance. They wanted everyone to behave just as they usually did, so that they could really learn something about us. This struck the boys of the area as a new rave scene. With all that free booze and pot how could it be anything else? They took a basement in the area and stocked it up on the Hausers' money.

By the time I arrived at the party it was reeking with enough marijuana to send a vice squad into orgasms of joy, there was liquor all over the place and the blare of the jazz would blow a hole in your head. All the hustlers were having a ball. But the do-gooders had withdrawn into a corner where they were sitting being stiffly polite. Someone was offering Mrs Hauser a draw and she was smiling sweetly and saying: 'I don't smoke.' Others were watching with fixed, aloof expressions. They didn't want to partake, just observe—and God knows how they thought they'd really get to know about people by standing spiritual miles off and scanning the surface. There was unconscious insult in the attitude, too.

For some time the hustlers carried on swinging, enjoying themselves, and then suddenly a young Jamaican rounded on the waxworks in the corner and blasted off at them.

'What are you playing at?' he demanded. 'You say you want to meet people and we fix it up all nice and friendly and you don't want to meet anyone after all. You just want to sit there and gawp like we're zoo animals. Well fuck that game! We don't dig it! You just join in or find yourselves another party.' This quote is approximate since he was rather strong in his language. He was genuinely hurt by their attitude and since his view was quite clearly shared by all the other hustlers, the do-gooders realised they had no option but to join the fun.

Once the decision was made and acted on, they were half paralysed and looking partly human in no time. From then on the party went like a rocket and we had a great time observing their interesting behaviour.

How much this party actually helped the Hausers with their subsequent meetings and research I wouldn't pretend to know, but it set the pattern for other groups who wanted to get to know us.

Among these was a party of M.P.'s who wanted to see something of the native of Notting Hill in his natural habitat. It was arranged that a friend and I should show them around and I had a meeting with them to describe what we had to offer. They were fascinated by the underworld picture I painted and decided the places where they could best acquire a closer knowledge of the area and its people were the illicit drinking and smoking clubs— the shebeens.

At first I was a little sceptical about taking such custodians of the country's values on a conducted tour of our subversive sub-strata, but they convinced me that there would be no come-backs and that it was all in the nature of research. So I talked the owner of one of the shebeens into receiving them.

The club was a large basement which members would nor-mally approach with circumspection. We rolled up to it like a royal procession in three large gleaming cars which the M.P.'s insisted should take them right to the door and remain parked smack outside like a convoy. They were laughing and joking and thoroughly excited about their bit of slumming. Inside the club, where everyone had been warned to relax, the occupants were doing their best to be casual. A couple of guys were rolling weed on a table, others were drinking at the bar and a number of prostitutes were hanging around hoping to pick up clients.

I introduced my companions to a few people, including the very nervous owner, and one of the M.P.'s asked if he could buy a drink. The owner glanced at me dubiously and I gave him a nod figuring we might as well be hanged for a sheep as a lamb. He didn't buy *a* drink. He bought drinks all round, setting the pattern for the rest of the visitors. Someone started the juke box and the ladies began gravitating towards the M.P.'s who looked like being real spending gentlemen.

The ice was broken in no time at all and in a little longer everyone was everyone else's very best friend. One of the prosti-tutes began demonstrating how to roll a marijuana cigarette, the West Indians began to expound on how happy they had been to have all the do-gooding ladies looking into their problems and the beaming landlord expatiated on his pleasure at finally getting the better class of people into his club. There was music, dancing, laughter, ribaldry. It was a beautiful evening. By the time I left in the early hours of the morning, the M.P.'s had dwindled to two. The other four had long since drifted off—presumably to acquire a better knowledge of the area and its people.

Not much good may have come of this particular bit of re-search, but no harm came of it either. The club didn't get busted,

as some of us had feared it might. And the owner still has his
dreams of glory.

In the midst of these somewhat abortive affairs, there was one
point the various do-gooding groups kept coming up with. It was
accurate if not exactly revolutionary : much of the area's problems arose from the shocking overcrowding.

One rather interesting example was that of a middle-aged
Barbadian woman, who lived with her husband and two sons
in a flat with three bedrooms. This should have been a nice scene,
but the number of occupants started to increase, with each son
acquiring a girl friend and one of them having two children. At
this point, the mother decided to start taking care of local kids
while the parents were out at work. She did this for economic
reasons and the task was simplified by the fact that crèches run
by some of the local authorities were not adequate for the children of the area.

To make sure she did an efficient job and to make it nice for
the kids, this lady put in fifteen cots, which were filled forthwith.
Things appeared to be swinging until after a while the parents
started deserting the kids and she ended up like the Old Woman
who lived in a Shoe. She was also trying to accommodate a
woman who had moved in to help her with the children and what
with that houseful and nobody paying for half the kids, she found
everything too much and finally took off for the West Indies.

This was not typical, of course. No more so than the size of
the Irish family on the top floor of my building. A more normal
case would be that of a friend of mine who lived with an English
prostitute in a two-roomed flat. Everything was fine until she
started having babies. They ended up with five children, but
couldn't get anywhere more spacious to live.

During this period, my flat was something of a landmark for
the do-gooders due to the constant stream of visiting West Indians—and that was how I met the one man who really got
things moving.

He was a London County Councillor named Donald Chesworth, a large, fair-complexioned, slightly balding man in his
late thirties, who would be completely lost in a crowd. His
crumpled suit and unpolished shoes suggested his mind was on
more important things and when you talked with him you were
left in no doubt that it was. I was impressed by him from the

moment I met him in the makeshift office which was the front room of his flat in Cambridge Gardens. When he talked, he looked me straight in the eyes and I found his concern and his determination to get things done quite compelling. He told me he wanted to do something about the wretched conditions we lived in throughout the area, but that he needed some co-operation from the residents if he was to succeed. I liked him and said I would help him in any way I could. In fact, the first night I met him I must have got quite carried away because I spent about four hours telling him about things that were wrong—everything I could think of, from the squalor the Irish lived in to the fact that my drain was blocked and flooding the basement area with stagnant water.

Early the following morning I conducted him on a tour to show him some of the things I'd been talking about and I introduced him to the Irish, navigating through a sea of 2,000 unwashed milk bottles on their landing to do so.

By midday the drain—which I'd spent days trying to induce the authorities to clear—was functioning perfectly and the milk bottles had all disappeared from the landing. This was a very impressive introduction to Mr Chesworth's ability to get things done and I began to see more of him.

On his suggestion I registered at the Labour Exchange in an effort to give up hustling. I duly received £8 10s a week benefit, which barely covered my rent. When I explained this little difficulty, he started to tell me about rent tribunals. I told him that Rachman appeared to be the only landlord willing to rent to black people and I would find it very hard to take someone that sympathetic to a rent tribunal. I remember he fixed those dead straight eyes on me and handed me a map with rings round the hundred and forty-seven properties Rachman owned in the area.

'The reason he owns all those places is because people like you have been paying him the money to buy them,' he said. 'I've been trying to do something about Rachman for a long time, but it seems everyone's afraid of him.'

'I'm not afraid,' I said. 'It's just that I'm thankful to have somewhere to live and he's providing it.'

'Do you want to live like an animal all your life?' he retorted. And I suddenly felt ashamed and promised I would talk to Desirée about it.

It wasn't easy to talk to Desirée about it. She was happy with where we were living for the first time since we'd been together. She was pregnant, too, and happy about that. And we had started talking about getting married. All this was suddenly put in jeopardy by the possibility of taking a wrong step. Desirée's first question was whether we were likely to lose the flat by taking Rachman to the rent tribunal and I told her that Mr Chesworth had said we would get a term of security of tenure which could be renewed.

'Do you believe him?' she asked.

'Yes,' I said. 'I do.'

Breaking Rachman began to emerge as one of Donald Chesworth's major ambitions and when he saw we were interested, he asked me if I could get some of my friends to join me. I spoke to Nick, who was also living in a Rachman property, and to Woodley and a number of others. They were not keen on getting involved. It was their view that all the do-gooders would clear off in the end leaving us to face the music as before. But Woodley suggested we test Chesworth, just to see how deep his interest in helping us went.

We had a couple of friends in trouble with the police at the time. They had been wrongfully arrested, but didn't know what to do about it. We told Chesworth that if he did something for them then we would do something about his plan.

His answer was typical of the man. He said quite categorically that he would not make bargains, but that if the two young men had, in fact, been wrongfully arrested, he would want to do something about it anyway. He got lawyers working on it immediately and arranged for prison visits. One of the two men was released within a few days. And inquiries began to proceed about the other.

That was enough for us. We voted wholehearted support for Chesworth against Rachman.

Chesworth's plan was to get every single Rachman tenant to go to the rent tribunal and thus make a clean sweep of the area. We were to visit all our friends and win them over to this idea. It was the sort of persuasion they'd never accept from a white man.

We got to work, calling on tenants whose names he gave us. And very uphill work it was. Rachman's tenants were frightened people. Apart from the insecurity engendered in them by their position as second-class citizens, they all knew that Rachman was one of the very few landlords who'd rent to black people.

They also knew about his 'right hand men' and the dogs—no small deterrent for people who recognised from experience that they could expect little protection from the police.

However, we worked hard, convincing people first and then instructing them how to fill in the application forms we carried with us. Eventually we had about thirty, which, on current canvassing, was the most we could expect. Among them was my own.

A couple of days later I had visitors. I opened the door of my flat in answer to a knock and found myself face to face with four tough-looking young Polish guys. With my hand on the door, I asked them what they wanted and one, who acted as spokesman, asked me why I was taking my landlord to the rent tribunal. He didn't adopt an aggressive or threatening tone, so instead of slamming the door on them, I replied that my rent was too high and I couldn't pay it. He asked me how much I earned and I told him—£8 10s National Assistance.

'Who told you to do it?' he asked.

'It's my own doing,' I said.

'All right,' he said. 'Drop your application and we will arrange for your rent to be reduced.'

Donald Chesworth had already warned me this might happen and that if I went along with it I'd have no security of tenure and they could throw me out any time they chose.

'I'll think about it,' I said.

'There's nothing to think about,' the Pole insisted. 'We'll reduce your rent to £6 a week, which is very reasonable. All you have to do is sign this sheet saying you'll withdraw your application.'

'I'll discuss it with my wife and let you know,' I said.

At this point another of them broke in.

'We haven't got time to be running around,' he said. 'We've been nice to your people for a long time and we don't want trouble.'

'I'm sorry,' I said. 'I have to discuss it first.'

'I'd advise you to sign it right now,' he said.

I didn't like his manner, which was menacing, and I didn't answer.

'How much are they paying you to do this?' he demanded.

His tone was getting rougher and it put my back right up.

'You can all fuck off,' I said. 'And if you want to get rough you can try what you like.'

We stood staring at one another for several seconds and then the first man told the others : 'Let's go,' and added that he'd like to come back and see me again. They went off taking the withdrawal sheet with them and I called Donald Chesworth immediately. He said he wanted to see me anyway and would I come to his office bringing my friends with me. When I reached his flat with Nick, Woodley and the rest of the boys, he produced a whole host of application withdrawals.

'They've been flooding in,' he said. 'They're all written with the same typewriter. This is intimidation and I'd like you to talk to someone from Scotland Yard.'

For people in the ghetto the police are the enemy, with Scotland Yard as the staff corps. The idea of talking to them was anathema to me and I said we'd have to think of something else. I had to admit that the possibility of withdrawing my own application had arisen in my mind. When I said this Chesworth became quite upset.

'That's the kind of thing that happens constantly in an area like this,' he said. 'It's what keeps it the way it is. The people won't stand up for themselves. They have no guts.'

He made me feel rather ashamed. He'd done all he'd promised since I'd met him and I didn't want to let him down.

'Don't worry,' I said. 'Whatever happens I won't withdraw now'.

It seemed that of thirty-three applications twenty-nine had been withdrawn. Nick, Woodley, another guy and I were the only ones sticking it out. Chesworth tried to persuade us to have police protection, but we said we'd rather protect ourselves and then he suggested that I, as main organiser, should have one of his subordinates move into the flat with me until the application had been heard. He even came to the house and ate with us to talk Desirée into supporting this move.

And so one of his fellow workers, a man named Keith Lye, from Transport House, moved into our small front room. He was small, earnest and energetic and managed to give a completely false impression that he didn't know what was happening. He stayed with us twenty-four hours a day, he and his typewriter, and whenever we went out he went with us. I can't say I felt any more secure for his presence, but it turned out to be fun. Keith was just a tiny bit square when he joined us, but in no time he was eating hot foods and doing all the things we did. I

swear his Establishment accent took on a slight West Indian
lilt.

During the time he was with us, he would answer the telephone and often nobody would speak—a procedure he put down
to Rachman's nerve-war methods. But the only real trouble we
had during that time was when we tried to take Keith into local
clubs. They all thought he was a cop.

The day came for my application to be heard and we all went
to the West London Rent Tribunal. It was a pure formality. My
rent was reduced to £4 a week, Nick's from £6 to £2 and the
others had similar cuts.

We were jubilant about the principle of the thing, though in
practical terms, having £4 10s a week to live on didn't raise us
to subsistence level.

After the cheers had died down, I told Donald Chesworth that
I couldn't go on working with him indefinitely, that I had to get
a job or I'd soon be flat broke. He understood that I was referring
to hustling, since I'd been reporting regularly to the Labour
Exchange for work which never materialised. He was very sympathetic and told me he'd see what he could do about it. As
usual he kept his word and the next time I went to the Exchange
they sent me to the National Assistance Office, where I was given
a cheque for £26 which they said was back payment for my not
having been allowed enough in the first place. My weekly assistance was increased to £9 2s 6d at the same time.

On the strength of this, Desirée and I made a decision and got
a marriage licence. And as if it were all part of a plan, a couple
of days later I was offered a job as a painter. It was the only job
the Exchange had ever held out to me and I was very surprised.
In fact, the day I went in and they sent me upstairs with a little
card instead of downstairs to sign for my money, I thought it
could only be something bad and expected them to tell me I
wasn't qualified for any more bread.

By the time Desirée and I got married three weeks later, I was
a very respectable, five-day-week worker in a nice, straight occu-
pation.

I'm afraid the job didn't last long. I found it was not, in fact,
painting. All I was doing was washing down walls for the painter.
Also, I was paid £10 a week, which meant that by the time I'd
spent money on fares and had National Insurance stamps and
tax deducted, I was worse off than I had been on National

Assistance. In short, I was working like hell at something very unsatisfying for less than I could get for doing nothing. I packed it in and went back on the register.

With time on my hands once again, I went back into business with Donald Chesworth. He hadn't been having very much success. As fast as applications went in they were withdrawn, for reasons that were only too obvious. But this time we organised more efficiently.

First of all I would visit houses in the area with some of the boys and explain the advantages of applying to the tribunal, quoting myself as an example of someone who'd had his rent reduced and suffered no ill effects from it. To add strength to this, I'd tell the tenants that some of us were forming a sort of vigilante patrol and that if they had any threats from thugs we'd take care of it. This was the sort of language they understood. After we'd finished, Chesworth and his student helpers would follow in our footsteps explaining the operation in greater detail.

We worked hard for three months, during which time we collected two hundred and forty applications. Everything went smoothly and more than two hundred resulted in rent reductions.

As joint organiser of this operation, I was paid expenses by Chesworth and these, added to National Assistance, provided me with enough to live on. We were beginning to have a little social life, too, going with Donald Chesworth to an Indian restaurant occasionally—and Desirée was very happy about that. She was looking very beautiful. I am terribly kinky for pregnant women and she looked like a pretty little round dumpling, which knocked me out.

In the middle of this swinging period in which I really felt I was doing something useful and life was opening out a bit, I had a visit from Rachman in person.

I was returning home at night and had reached the basement steps when a man emerged from the shadows of the house next door and said : 'We would like to talk to you.'

At that instant I noticed a car parked at the kerb a little way off, with the door opening and someone getting out. I knew immediately that it was Rachman. When I had met him before, he'd just looked like an ordinary little landlord collecting rent, but now, in the light of our operation and all the stories I'd heard about him, he had a completely different dimension. Even his physical appearance seemed to carry an aura of sinister power.

Two more big men got out of the car with him and they all came silently over to the basement steps.

This was the one occasion when I didn't have Nick and Woodley with me. You can't panic in a situation like that. You have to go along with the game no matter what's going to happen.

'All right,' I said. 'Come on in.'

They followed me into the flat and Desirée stared at us, frightened.

'These gentlemen want to talk to me,' I said.

She looked from them to me as if she was ready to scream and I put my hand on her and said : 'It's all right. Don't worry. They just want to talk.'

I took them into the little front room and asked them to sit down and offered them coffee. They looked at one another and Rachman said : 'Sure—thanks very much.'

When Desirée had gone off reluctantly to make the coffee, Rachman looked me straight in the eyes and said : 'Your name is Michael?'

'Yes,' I said.

He nodded and went on : 'I've heard quite a lot about you lately. You've been creating quite a bit of bother , . . making a nuisance of yourself.'

He spoke quite flatly, without anger and I didn't answer, just sat listening to what he had to say.

He began to tell me how, many years ago, he'd come to the area as an immigrant and hadn't been able to get anywhere to live, how he'd made money and started buying up houses and sub-letting them, how he intended no harm to anyone and how his property was the only property in the area where black people could live—which was true.

The three-man bodyguard sat watching me without expression throughout his speech and Desirée reappeared in the doorway and stood listening. When he stopped talking, Rachman looked at her and now that things were calmer I formally introduced her to him. His manner was quite mild and pleasant and he asked if this was our first child and whether we wanted a girl or a boy. Apart from the rather forbidding presence of his henchmen, the meeting began to take on the atmosphere of a tea party. And then he suddenly asked me if I worked with Chesworth and I said I helped him.

'What's in it for you?' Rachman asked.

'I don't really know,' I said.

He began to give me a long spiel: 'You're a young boy and I will tell you a few things. All these people will want you to do things for them—they're all making a lot of money. And you have a wife and a second child coming and you don't have any money and never will the way you're going on. When these councillors and people have got their publicity and the other things they want, they'll leave, but you'll still be here and I'll be the only one renting you a house. So why pressure me in this way?'

I didn't have any answer for him. He managed to make me feel a little guilty.

At this point my little daughter, Jennifer, came toddling into the room and Rachman picked her up and played with her, which all added to his air of humanity and charm. He told me he had other houses outside the area and asked if I'd like to move, giving weight to the proposition by adding: 'You can't go on living here in two rooms if you're going to have a couple of children.'

I said I didn't know that I wanted to move, with my rent now only £4.

'You'll go on paying £4 a week,' he said. 'I don't want to interfere with your rent.'

Desirée and I looked at each other. I didn't know what attitude to adopt. Or what the alternatives were that he was offering. He went on playing with Jennifer as if it were just as important that she should be amused as it was that our conversation should continue.

'Will you call this thing off that you're doing?' he asked.

'Why should I?' I said.

'I'll get you somewhere to live,' he said, 'and I'll give you your first stake and a job where you can earn some money.'

'Whether I move or you move me, what's happening is not going to stop,' I said. 'It's going on anyway.'

'That's up to me,' he replied. 'I'll decide that. What I want to know is if you'll take my offer.'

'I'll think about it,' I said.

He seemed to accept that. He handed me a card with the address of his new office in Westbourne Grove.

'I'll expect you in the morning,' he said. 'You can tell me then.'

He and his men began to leave, passing the kitchen where the forgotten coffee kettle had burnt out on the gas. Rachman saw it and leapt inside to turn off the burner.

'You've lost your kettle,' he said to Desirée.

He put his hand in his pocket, brought out a five-pound note and held it out to her, saying : 'Buy a new one.'

Desirée suddenly burst into tears. He tried to press the note on her, but she wouldn't put out her hand to take it. Crying, she turned her back on him and walked away. I said : 'Just go,' and opened the door for them to leave.

After they'd gone, I sat with Desirée and calmed her and she said : 'There's going to be trouble.'

'There's been trouble all the time,' I said. 'It's nothing new.'

I didn't go to Rachman's office next morning, but by midday a man came to the door bearing a note from him and a beautiful little kettle. The note said : 'Sorry for the distress I caused you. Please accept this little present.'

So we were a kettle up.

Strangely enough I didn't hear from Rachman again. Rents were reduced and he and his people appeared to cool off. We thought, naturally, that it was because we were too strong for him —but, looking back, I'm not so sure. . . .

Rachman was a very clever man and he and other landlords adopted two different methods to deal with the pressure which was put on them. The first was simply to sell their properties— giving first option to the sitting tenants—at a very high price. They would arrange 100 per cent mortgages through a building society and sell £3,000 houses for £4,500. The people in the area, given the first chance in their lifetime of owning their houses, saw no option but to purchase.

The second method was to sell a leasehold on the property at a price which would more than cover the overall value and yet retain the freehold. Again 100 per cent mortgages were granted and some very interesting fortunes made. I remember one house on Colville Terrace, which was worth £3,000 before Rachman was pressured. It contained five flats and he sold the leasehold of each for £750, making a total of £3,750. The lease reverted to him after twelve years.

Rachman did all this in a crash programme. What it amounted to was that when his return on capital—namely rents—was cut down, he simply increased the capital by selling. It wasn't such a good long-term proposition, but it was a very profitable alternative for him in the circumstances.

He was certainly right about one thing : the do-gooders, apart from Chesworth, didn't stay long. We tried desperately at that time to show the world the vicious conditions people lived in throughout the area—but few were really interested. We were just a pack of niggers living in bad houses—so what?

There are quite a few things one can say about Peter Rachman. I think he had a rather unfortunate deal. True he was charging a lot for his houses, but it turned out he wasn't the only one. There are bigger fish in the area than him.

Rachman's name became a household word due to his connection with Mandy Rice-Davies and Christine Keeler and so Rachmanism became an adjective in the English language. Poor Peter Rachman—going down to posterity like that. He was a businessman like any other. He wanted to make money and he provided a service which was badly needed. He charged exorbitant rents, but if it hadn't been for him a lot of black people would have slept in the streets. He used toughs to collect the rents, but it's the usual thing to hire awful bastards to do awful jobs. The police force doesn't attract the best people either.

I'm not eager to run to his defence. But I object to him being used as a scapegoat to conscience in this country. The real villain was not Peter Rachman. It was, and still is, all those who put up notices saying : 'no coloured' . . . 'no Irish' . . . 'no children' . . . 'no dogs' . . . the 'no' people : nasty, mean, ignorant, joyless people. They're the ones who made it possible for Rachman to provide his particular kind of service. They and the well-meaning people who condemn him but do nothing about the situation that created him.

Don't forget, the English made the atmosphere which allowed Rachman to ply his trade. If you want the true adjective for the dictionary, you can cut out Rachmanism and put in Englishism. That's a much more vicious thing.

11

Ever since setting up house in the ghetto, I had kept up a rambling correspondence with my mother and when I wrote and told her I was married she wrote back to say she was thinking of coming over here. I panicked immediately and sent back a long letter to discourage her. England, I said, was not the place for her. It was a country where people worked hard—and she wasn't young any more. I didn't have room for her. And anyway I was thinking of returning to the West Indies eventually.

To my horror, her answer to this was another letter in which she said she had put up her house for sale and was definitely coming as she wanted to take care of her future grandchildren.

Desperation moved me. I sent a cable to Trinidad telling her there were problems of race in this country, that her coming was a very, very bad idea, that she shouldn't dream of coming under any conditions. I also sent off letters to friends and relatives telling them to put her off at all costs. I breathed a sigh of relief and sat back thinking I really had things under control now and that would be the end of it.

The next letter I received said that her passage had been booked on such and such a boat and she would be arriving on such and such a date. In great consternation I found the boat had already left before I got the letter. There was just no stopping my mother once she decided to do something.

The first thing I did was talk to Desirée, telling her exactly what kind of woman my mother was, preparing her for the

trouble in store. 'What will you do with her?' Desirée asked.
'What can I do but let her stay here for a few weeks,' I said. 'We
can have a talk and maybe she'll decide to go back. If not I'll
find her somewhere else to live.'

My mother came by the immigrants' boat to Genoa and then
overland to London. A Dominican friend, James, and I went to
meet her at Waterloo. It was a hot summer day and the usual
mad scene at the station—lots of black families meeting their
kin, pickpockets, case-snatchers . . . I had been describing her to
James as we walked along the platform and we went the whole
length of the train without a sign of her. I was just telling him,
'It doesn't look like she came,' and feeling very relieved when I
heard an unmistakeable voice screaming, 'Mikeeee!' 'That's my
mother,' I said, and we turned and saw her standing by a carriage
in a bright red quilted bathrobe. Some wicked person in Trinidad
had sold her this, telling her it was an overcoat and that she'd
need it in England. She looked a sight.

I was very embarrassed and grabbed her by the arm while
she tried to introduce me to everyone on the train. I hauled her
away and bundled her into a cab. I was so intent on getting the
hell out of there that it wasn't until I'd given the cabbie directions
that I realised she was shouting, 'What about my suitcases—my
clothes?' And we had to make a colourful, blushing, sortie onto
the platform to get them.

The taxi driver started giving us a grand tour, thinking we were
all immigrants, but I didn't mind as I was able to point out a few
landmarks for my mother and distract her from her obvious dis-
comfiture that I was accompanied by a black friend rather than
a white.

When we finally reached the house, Desirée was there to meet
us, dressed in her best and looking very nervous. My mother
looked right past her as if she didn't exist. I said: 'This is my
wife.' My mother halted dead in her tracks at my words and her
mouth sagged open and her face fell. I had completely forgotten
to tell her I was married to a black woman.

My mother looked so shocked and horrified that Desirée began
to cry. It was a terrible opening scene.

I ushered my mother through to her room, where she immediately pulled a bottle of rum from her suitcase and said: 'Let's
get drunk.' She and James began to act on that, while Desirée
made coffee to steady her nerves. Eventually the two women ex-

changed a few words about sleeping arrangements and then my mother passed out.

Life from then on was impossible. My mother told me later that she was so surprised to see so many black people in London that she almost fainted on arrival. It had never occurred to her I would not be married to an English girl and it took her days to recover from the shock. Once she did, she tried to take over the house . . . from breakfast time on. She would tell Desirée exactly what I did and didn't like. If Desirée was grilling me chops, my mother would quickly remove them from the grill and throw them in a pot, saying: 'He doesn't like them that way. He only likes them stewed.'

Desirée was afraid to complain to me at first. She would just sit and cry and I couldn't understand why she was crying and got furious. Then gradually the arguments began to come out into the open and I got caught up in the crossfire. The climax came over a paraffin heater. My mother would turn up the one in her room to its highest possible point so that it smoked and smelt awful. Desirée would turn it down and my mother would turn it up again since they were quite unable to communicate with each other. One day Desirée came screaming from my mother's room: 'Your mother wants to catch the house on fire! You've got to do something with her!' I went into the room and sure enough the paraffin heater was blazing away. I told my mother to turn it down as it was too high and likely to explode and she screamed at me in turn: 'She wants you to make me cold!' I tried to explain the workings of a paraffin heater to her and she retorted: 'She won't let me do anything in my own house.'

Something had to be done and I insisted we sat down for a serious chat, but my mother leapt into the attack, declaring she was going to move out. I said this was a big decision and it would take us a while to find somewhere. She said: 'Don't worry, I'll be gone this evening.' And she began to pack.

That evening she moved out to stay with some black friends she'd made in the three weeks she'd been with us. They lived just up the street and they immediately stopped talking to Desirée because of the terrible stories they began to hear about her. It took me a day or two to get life in my own home back to normal and then I began calling in on my mother to see if there was anything I could do. She'd been away no more than a week when I looked in during her absence and her friends told me she was having a £12 a week flat redecorated in Elgin Crescent and was preparing to move in. I was amazed. It was a two-bedroom place, much bigger than mine. I felt there must be some mistake.

I saw my mother and asked her if it was true she was moving.

'Yes,' she said. 'Soon as it's ready.'

'But why do you want such a large place?' I asked.

'I like a bit of space,' she said.

'And how the devil you going to pay for it?'

'Don't you worry. I'll get along.'

Her complete confidence unnerved me and I didn't ask any more questions.

In a few days my mother moved and the mystery was solved. She simultaneously took on a tenant—a prostitute, who used the second bedroom as a hustling gaff and paid £3 a day rent.

That was just the beginning. From that point on my mother gradually built up a little hustling empire over the years. She rented a number of flats and had up to fifteen prostitutes working for her. She mixed these with a number of straight tenants as protection against the police. If she got word that a particular flat was being observed she would transfer people to make it a respectable establishment. Her tenants were constantly being evicted and rehoused, amidst protests, around the corner somewhere. She was a cool operator.

At the same time, she managed to start building up a far-flung obeah business. She began with the gamblers in the ghetto, giving them some magic power to win, and eventually men were coming from as far away as Birmingham and Manchester for a fifteen-minute interview which would cost them £30-£40.

I was there once when she saw a gambler. He sat on a chair in her chaotic room looking sad, while she reclined, all muffled up against the English weather she hated, in her bed.

'What's wrong son?' she said.

'I lost all my money,' he said.

My mother talked to him for ten minutes about his past life and what he was doing now and then she said: 'Are you going to gamble tonight?'

He nodded and she took a £5 note and a cheap little charm such as you might find in a Christmas cracker from a bedside drawer.

'Put the charm in your pocket and start with the note,' she said. 'And come back here with half your winnings.'

D

He went happily away and returned the next day with £60 for my mother. She looked him in the eye and said: 'What's that?' 'I won,' he replied. My mother waved the notes away. 'How can you lie to me when I was with you all the time?' she demanded. The guy began begging her to take it, but she sent him packing, telling him, 'You're going to need it.'

That man admitted to me later that it was not an even split and said he'd been flat broke ever since. He begged me to talk to my mother for him. I asked her what she was doing to the poor guy and she just said: 'He's confused. He gonna lose from now on.' He has.

The gamblers had implicit faith in my mother's power and it's true that if she turned them on they won. I think this was very much to do with their belief that they were going to win once they'd seen her. A successful gambler really needs a lot of confidence and quite a bit of bravado. He has to be bold and not allow himself to become hesitant and confused. My mother's clients were the most bold and confident men in the world.

My mother really loved this whole hustling scene and the prostitutes were wild about her. They thought she was the most wonderful woman in Notting Hill and were very loyal.

There was Connie, an old bag of a woman with teenage children, a small, thin, hard-featured redhead. She was terribly downtrodden when my mother took her over. She was earning only £10 a day and male hustlers were taking nearly all of it away from her. My mother virtually adopted her. She sharpened her up and took complete charge of her money, leaving her simply to concern herself with the actual hustling, which was all she wanted to do. My mother gave her full protection. The hustlers who had been taking her money were terrified of the power of the obeah and left her alone at a word from my mother. Connie worked harder and her earnings doubled. She ended up with a savings bank account arranged by my mother, a place to live in and anything she wanted. She called my mother 'Mummy' and seemed really happy for probably the first time in her life. She got into the habit of cleaning the house and running errands to show her appreciation and at my mother's funeral a while back she cried genuine tears because something rather beautiful had gone from her life.

So devoted to my mother were these ladies that one of them, Iris, a plump English Jewess, was quite jealous about the chores

Connie did and was always trying to take them over. She believed very strongly in spiritualism and reincarnation and my mother had many long talks with her on the subject. A few days before my mother died, she told Iris it was going to happen very soon and that she would communicate with her through me. Iris has been badgering me ever since, which is a terrible drag as I don't want her around and, what's more, I haven't had any messages for her.

During her long hustling career here, my mother was only busted once.

I had a telephone call from a friend, saying: 'Have you heard what's happened with your mother?' 'No,' I said. 'Well you'd better come down here quickly,' he said. 'No,' I said, 'tell me what's happened.' 'Come down here right away,' he said and hung up.

Desirée and I were living in Islington at the time and we got into the car and drove like maniacs to Notting Hill to learn that my mother had been arrested for running a brothel. I was very angry and embarrassed as I was trying hard to go straight, but I got on the phone and did the usual things like calling lawyers.

Next day when she appeared in court and was fined some small sum, which she paid on the spot, I discovered she'd given her name as De Freitas—which it had never been.

'Why did you do that—and how could you?' I asked.

'I had to give some name,' she replied, 'and I didn't want to spoil my own.' She never really gave a damn about me.

My mother ended her days in a three-bedroomed flat in St Stephen's Gardens, lording it over her prostitutes and a group of little old ladies, who looked as if they came out of the woodwork and were completely fascinated by her. They would sit around her bed in her crummy little room, watching television and attending to her every whim until the early hours of the morning. What they really wanted was to go to Trinidad with her and I think she fed their dreams. Most of them were charladies, but they soon gave that up and just sat around all day listening to my mother, cooking for her and acting as receptionists for the gamblers, telling them, 'I'm afraid you can't see her now,' when she became temperamental and didn't want to be disturbed.

My mother liked these little old ladies very much. When she suddenly went on a pilgrimage to Lourdes shortly before she died, she actually took one of them with her—a funny little old soul who'd never before left England and never expected to.

For an old lady who hardly left her bed, my mother wielded an incredible amount of power in Notting Hill. She had the sort of power that made strong friends and strong enemies—like the young men who wrote her an anonymous letter threatening to beat her up, 'if not this week, next week, or some time in the future. . . .' The letter was said to come from some of her evicted tenants, but they never dared try to put their words into action.

Since her death, I've heard how her power even extended to give me protection. People have told me: 'Nobody in here would tamper with you, man. They too terrified of your mother.'

She let it be known before she died that all her power was going to me. I knew nothing of this until a Barbadian approached me in Reading a little while ago and asked me with great reverence if my name was Michael. He then told me he used to talk to my mother and he asked me for some 'powder', offering me a £10 note. The powder, I discovered, was for his wife. She was threatening to leave him and he was convinced that if he gave her this powder in a drink she wouldn't go. I told him I didn't have any powder and didn't want his money. 'Go home and talk to your wife,' I said. 'Tell her how you really feel.' I figured that would do him much more good. Perhaps it would even solve their problems, in which case, nobody would ever be able to tell him I hadn't inherited my mother's powers.

There's no doubt my mother had a type of beauty which was recognised by weak people because of the strength in it. She had this ability to convince people she could do things for them through obeah. They believed every word and they went away happier. As long as they believed, the job was done. I was too close to her to have any respect for these divine powers. I saw her as a mortal with a lot of unpleasant aspects. But I also admired her a lot in a way. I admired her energy. Lots of people have ideas, but it's the doers who really make it and she managed to do everything she said she would, no matter how misguided.

At her funeral, the grave was surrounded by weeping prostitutes, hustlers and gamblers. That was her scene. I don't think there was anything anyone could have done to change that woman. It might not have been wise to try. For she was certainly happy in her way.

12

Towards the end of the Rachman business I found myself mixed up in an organisation scene for the first time. Someone turned up from a body called the 'Coloured People's Progressive Association' and gave me a little card saying I was a vice-chairman.

I was quite surprised, but I went to their committee meeting and discovered Woodley was a member and had nominated me, telling them: 'Get Michael involved and you'll get things done.'

Not much happened beyond introductions at the committee meeting. Everybody was clearly very well intentioned and the organisation had good general aims of improving the lot of the coloured people in the area. A full meeting to include ordinary members was called for the following day. When I turned up to this, I found to my horror that there were thirty white people present and only nine black.

As a new vice-chairman I was called on, with pleasurable expectation, to make a speech. I stood up and made one. I said I didn't think any black organisation should have all those white people in it. As it stood, it couldn't be called a black organisation; it was just a white take-over. The pleasurable expectation soured in a flash. I could see the faces freezing over as I spoke and by the time I sat down I was the least popular person present by several hundred per cent. I learned of my dismissal through the local paper a few days later.

The organisation crumbled not long afterwards and years later when I met the chairman, he said to me: 'You were right.' He had found it was simply impossible to have all those whites in a black organisation. He couldn't involve the black people in what was happening, because the white members were doing it all. He ended up with a near all-white organisation.

This happens in nearly all the so-called coloured organisations. You find a lot of white liberals doing all the work. They are very kind and efficient; they take care of the secretarial side; they raise funds; they have a great organisation going. But it's a white organisation. The black man doesn't learn a thing from it. Everything is done for him.

The white liberals are, in fact, destroying the black man. They help to foster his ignorance because he never has the opportunity to learn. I sometimes feel the white liberal must know this. He must, surely. He's an educated man.

Certainly, I recognise that white people can be used in a black organisation—in the background. Or they could do an excellent job going out among their own people who are riddled with prejudice. One never sees these articulate white ladies and gentlemen who get involved with black people moving around their own comfortable areas telling their white neighbours that they don't know how to treat black men. They prefer to be in the ghetto telling the black man how awful it is the way he's treated and how very much they sympathise. In the long run they don't really help at all.

Around this time, Desirée had our child—a daughter we named Kerine Michelle—and I decided I had to do something to make more money. The rent tribunals were still dragging on, but the do-gooders were leaving the area and I was somewhat disenchanted with their lack of real interest.

The last straw for me was when Chesworth wanted a playground for the area. The boys and I helped him and we found and cleared a site on a piece of waste ground. Chesworth had to fight tooth and nail to get a grant from the local council to pay for a caretaker. He then brought in a titled lady to be one of the founder members and when they saw this, some of those local bigwigs who'd been anything but keen on the idea immediately leapt in and started carrying on as if the whole thing were their doing. One lady who came in at the very last meeting, after we'd done everything, began making statements to the press about 'my playground'. Most of these people were not really concerned about doing good; they were just out for personal glory. I told them so at a meeting and walked out. It was the wrong thing for me to do and I learned from it that if you don't like the way things are being done, stay with them and change them from the inside. You can't do it from outside.

So I went back to hustling. I opened a gaming house with another guy in a basement in Powis Terrace. That may sound rather grand, but, in fact, all you need is a large table covered in baize, with pairs of dice, and a smaller table with cards, plus a few chairs. You make money by taxing the players, taking a percentage of whatever is bet.

Desirée didn't like the idea of my going back into hustling, but money talks, as they say. You can make £30 a week at these illicit places without working up a sweat. If you want to go at it really hard, you can make very much more. Altogether, I kept the gaming house close on two years with no attention from the police. Lots of clubs were raided, but they were bigger establishments. I kept mine small enough just to make sufficient money for my family.

When I was picked up by the police, it was for something quite different.

I was walking along the street when a police car pulled up beside me and a couple of coppers got out and asked if I was Michael de Freitas and would I accompany them to the station. One doesn't argue with the police in Notting Hill and I went with them. At the station, to my total disbelief, I was charged with robbery with violence—with having beaten up a man, broken his arm and stolen the watch off his wrist. There wasn't even an identification parade. The guy whose arm had been broken, a little West Indian, materialised in the station and identified me, saying: 'Yes—you did it.'

I was flabbergasted. He compounded the injury by adding, yes, he'd known me for years and wasn't going to make a mistake; I'd done it all right.

I knew him vaguely, too. He was a Rachman tenant in St Stephen's Gardens where he ran a gaming house and dispensed drugs on the quiet. He claimed, apparently, that I walked in with another man when he was playing cards with some of his friends and started to beat him up. His friends were terrified and ran, while I broke his arm and took his watch.

I had no defence. It was supposed to have happened a few

days earlier and I couldn't even remember what I was doing then.

They took me to Brixton on remand for a week so that I had plenty of time to reflect on the fact that the offence carried a maximum penalty of seven years. Desirée and various friends came to visit me, begging me to tell them what I knew about it. What could I say? I knew nothing about it. I'd never done anything to the man or had any trouble with him.

People checked him for me and it turned out he actually was beaten up by someone and lost his watch in the process. Acting on this, my friends found the boy who beat him up. He was a young man from Trinidad who was serving in the Royal Air Force. He said he had been gambling and the game was crooked and he wanted his money back. That was what the fight had been about. He'd taken the watch as a recompense.

My friends saw the boy and explained the situation and asked him what he was going to do about it. His sister was telling him : 'Michael will get off, he's got friends, but you will be in for it,' and the boy was hesitating about what he should do. But then he had a long talk with Donald Chesworth and decided that it wasn't right that I should face seven years in prison for something he'd done—particularly since, with his story, he'd get a much shorter sentence. So he gave himself up at a police station and told the officer on duty all about it. Desirée had gone with him and she was adding her piece, saying : 'It's all a mistake about my husband and this boy wants to own up.'

The officer looked at the boy very straight and said : 'My son, we have nothing against you. You'd better get out of here pretty quick.' Desirée was crying and trying to remonstrate, but the two of them were virtually shooed out of the station.

The Trinidadian, whose unlikely name, by the way, was Innocent, had to return to base that weekend and he told his C.O. the story. The officer took him to the local police station, where, naturally, he was charged and returned to London. But I wasn't released and I bumped into him in Brixton Prison the very next day.

The situation now began to get very complicated. My accuser had all his witnesses ready to give evidence which would put me in gaol, but when they realised they might be held for perjury they began to disappear. He found himself with no witnesses, no case and somebody else in custody who was going to make

him out a liar. He did the only sensible thing in the circumstances
—promptly took off for the West Indies.

After I had spent two weeks in Brixton, Innocent and I
appeared in court, jointly charged. He pleaded guilty and told his
story once again.

The police, of course, denied that they'd refused to listen to
him and described his visit to the police station as complete fab-
rication. They took the view that I was a known figure in the
ghetto underworld, that three witnesses and the complainant had
disappeared and that foul play was suspected. What had really
happened was that they'd goofed. The case against me was dismissed.

I don't pretend to know what it was all about. But I do know
that I'd been bringing pressure to bear on people who mattered in
Notting Hill—like the landlords. And that would make anyone
pretty unpopular.

The West Indian who got me into this mess is back in Notting
Hill and he got messages to me to say that he was sorry. Veiled
messages, the way they are expressed in the ghetto—more like
feelers to see if it was safe for him to be back. It was safe enough.
I couldn't ask him for anything and there was no point in bearing a grudge. It was just something that happened. . . .

Quite a number of other things started happening around that
time. Among them was that I bought my first house and upset
quite a few people because of it. Like many others when the
house-selling market perked up, I decided I might as well have
a permanent place to live. I went to the building society principally involved and applied for a mortgage to buy a property
on Colville Terrace—one of Rachman's houses. It was a large,
typical terraced house and the price, like so many others, was
£4,500.

Even though they were handing out these mortgages all over
the place, I was the last sort of person to lend money to. I hadn't
had a regular job since I'd come to England. But in the building
society's offices somebody recognised me and whispered in someone else's ear and they said sign here and gave me the 100 per
cent mortgage on the spot. I was a little surprised at this, but it
wasn't that difficult to figure. By now I was recognised as something of a power in the area and they were interested in making
me a landlord, because landlords tend to cool down the fighting
tenants.

This was the view of the Powis and Colville Residents' Association which I had founded to help fight for the rights of tenants while I was working with Chesworth. I had moved off it, leaving an Englishman as secretary, acting, myself, only as adviser. I had always advocated including the landlords in the Association. That way the landlord *and* the tenant could be controlled, to the benefit of both parties. By now I was aware that quite a few problems were created by the tenants, that they could be at fault too. This had been brought home to me one day when a tenant complained that his ceiling was falling in and the landlord wouldn't do anything about it. When we saw the landlord, he said he'd just fixed the ceiling and it was the tenants' fault for doing their washing in the bathroom above. We investigated this and sure enough, there was an industrious Dominican lady washing all her clothes in a tub in the bathroom in the style of back home, scrubbing them on a board and slopping water all over the floor so that there was a great pool around her feet, constantly seeping through the floor below. . . .

Now the Association was filled with anxiety about my new role. They knew I had no money and then suddenly I had a house. There was quite a bit of envy in the air. I didn't let it worry me, though. I had a wife and daughters and I saw my transformation into a landlord as a natural development.

The four-storey house had two vacant floors and I moved into the top one which had five very large rooms. After years of living like a rat in basements, I wanted to be as high as possible. On reflection, the house was not the very best buy. There wasn't much income from it. But at least it was enough to pay the mortgage and the bills.

Fast on top of the acquisition of the house, a friend began to rent me his cottage in the country so that Desirée and the children could get away from the smoke of London for the weekends. And at the same time I started another gaming house in a friend's café in the East End.

The envious talk grew into a clamour. 'He's living very well,' they would say, as if they were suffering by it. It's true I was now living better than many people in Notting Hill, but I was working harder too.

The envy of the local residents had to find an outlet, of course, and it came with that unmistakable knocking on the door. I opened to the police and they told me I was being charged with running a brothel in the basement. I told them this was ridiculous, but they took me to the station and I appeared in court and was remanded in custody for a week. When I appeared before the magistrate, the police evidence was that they'd seen me collecting money from a prostitute at various times, but on some of these occasions I was actually in the country with my family. My lawyers called responsible people from the local village to give evidence rebutting the police and the case was dismissed.

As I was leaving court, having received justice, but financially much poorer, a police officer said quietly to me: 'You've won the first round, but I've been in the force twenty years and never lost a case and I'm not going to start now.'

It's true to say I've always had a very strange relationship with the police. They never managed to arrest me for any of the things I'd actually done; always for things I hadn't. Since I wasn't working most of the time, it was clear that I must be doing something outside the law. It was up to them to catch me and up to me not to get caught. All's fair in war, so if they got me on the wrong charges I couldn't really complain. It's every man for himself in the ghetto and some of the policemen they put in that area are the type who think black people are all savages. A black man starts with a built-in disadvantage, knowing that with such a policeman he can lose his freedom on any small whim. It's not uncommon in the Grove to pass a policeman on a corner and hear him grumble: 'Black bastard.'

In the ghettoes it's a big joke if any black man goes to the station to make a complaint. If it's not his day, he may very well be arrested and charged with disorderly conduct.

So if they tried a few low punches on us, it wasn't really surprising. Just another exercise in the fine art of suppressing the spirit of a people.

13

By this time I wanted to get out of the hustling scene. Out of Notting Hill. The pressure of the ghetto is always of a sort that pervades your very marrow and, for one reason or another, I was becoming too well known to the police. I felt as if I were being suffocated by the area. In a way I began to fear it.

In an attempt to escape, I sold the house in Colville Road at a profit of £900 and moved my family out to a flat in Stoke Newington. This removed me physically from the ghetto, but not mentally.

There seemed to be little I could do to go straight. I couldn't accept Richard Hauser's suggestion that he recommend me for training as a prison officer. I told him I'd somehow never seen myself on that side of the bars. Nor could I take the Labour Exchange with its 'no coloured' scene for this and that. I began to drift between Notting Hill and Stoke Newington, hustling during the day, returning to my family at night.

Desirée was pregnant again and began to badger me to give up hustling and do something with myself—go to school, back to sea, anything. She was dissatisfied with Stoke Newington, too. The people were all white and treated her with hostility. She said she was afraid walking in the streets at night and even wished she were back in Notting Hill where she felt safe. Certainly there was this anti-Jewish, anti-black atmosphere hanging over the whole area. I took off for Liverpool after a few weeks—having no stomach for the gaming houses—and signed on as an A.B with a Swedish vessel taking grain from the Russian Baltic ports. Almost as soon as I'd gone, Fascists who'd been painting swastikas all over Stoke Newington broke into the Jewish-owned house where my family lived and smashed everything up. Desirée, who was expecting our third child, was out at the clinic during the afternoon and she returned to find the back gate had been broken down and intruders had gained access to the house by smashing a window and coming in through the semi-basement flat we occupied. Banisters were ripped apart, mattresses torn to ribbons, pots and pans smashed all over the place. Among the things they stole were a new record player, a hair dryer, a load of my new shirts and a new suitcase to put them in. Anything they couldn't take they destroyed, even throwing plants out of pots. It was a hell of a scene for a woman living alone with her children to come back to and Desirée felt terribly nervous living there after that. So much for my efforts to find somewhere nicer to live.

I, in the meantime was in Russia, which, at first view, was Yugoslavia all over again only worse. I had this vision of the USSR as one vast military camp full of millions of men, guns, tanks and planes. Sure enough, when I actually tied up in Leningrad there was this military procedure with all the crew being lined up on deck and having their identities checked while the police and customs went through the ship with a fine-tooth comb. We also had to declare to the last detail any kind of currency we had and anything like a camera had to be placed in bond until the ship left. It was all very different from Western countries where the crew drifted around any old where while the customs were aboard, and things were pretty free and easy.

But at night when we went ashore, it was a more relaxed story. The first thing that happened as my shipmates and I walked through the streets was that we were discreetly approached by hordes of young Russian spivs wanting to buy everything from American dollars and English pounds to the coats off our backs. They spoke English well and although they were enthusiastic, they were also quite careful, walking apart from us and speaking over their shoulders like the Arab vendors one might meet in Port Said.

There was no bargaining because the prices they offered for everything were terribly good. They quoted prices for foreign exchange which were twice the official rate and apart from that they were very eager to buy anything nylon, from socks to shirts.

They also wanted Tommy Steele records and American pop music, overcoats and jackets. I was buying a lot of things to take home like Russian champagne, dolls and caviar—of which you could get a massive jar for a rouble, which was about three shillings. By the time evening came I had spent all my money and gave way to requests that I should sell the overcoat I was wearing. It was clean, but terribly old and a spiv gave me the equivalent of £45 for it as if I had done him a favour. On future trips I made sure I took a good selection of things they wanted. This provided me with a lot of bread to buy Russian goodies, which made for great champagne and caviar parties in the basement at Stoke Newington.

I found no racial prejudice in Russia. I might attract a few more stares than white sailors, but there was no animosity. Russia fell between Britain and Scandinavia in this respect. In Britain one wasn't wanted; in Scandinavia to be coloured was an asset with every lady following the usual sexual myth and wanting a black man; in Russia there was a sort of neutrality.

Not that I ever thought of Russia in sex terms, anyway. I and the rest of the crew always had the feeling there was no sex happening there.

In my first ten trips to the Soviet Union I saw only one prostitute—and I was so surprised to see that one that I didn't even recognise her. I was walking by the river in Leningrad one day when this not very attractive lady came up and spoke to me with what sounded like an American accent. She started to come on as if she wanted to pick me up and, since I had never seen a prostitute in Russia, I thought she was from another ship. I asked her which ship she was on and she said she wasn't from any, she lived there. She made me a proposition and wanted to take me off. She said: 'Follow me, but keep a little way behind me,' so doubtless she had to be as careful as the spivs. I was not very eager, however, and finally she went off with one of my friends. She didn't want money; she wanted clothes.

It was a very rare event for any visiting sailor to find a prostitute. There is a real absence of them in Russia. One of the few times I had a Russian woman, the circumstances were rather strange.

We had docked at a port on the Black Sea near Batumi, a resort not far from Odessa, and were kept there for a good ten days as we were loading oil and the Russians insisted on cleaning our tanks first as they were too dirty for the refined oil they wanted to put in them.

My favourite spot in Batumi was a pleasure boat just off the shore. It was like one of those old Mississippi ferryboats with two big open floors for dancing surrounded by tables, curtained cubicles and a capacious bar. The very first night I went in there with some friends from the ship, it was full of Russian men drinking and toasting one another and hugging one another the way Russians do. After a certain amount of vodka they all started doing Cossack dances, crouching and shooting their legs out parallel with the floor. My friends and I had been drinking quite well, too, and we started trying to do it with them. Whereas we might have made a good job of the limbo, this one was not our forte and we were falling all over the place with a lot of laughing and shouting, and finally the Russians were showing us how to do it, holding us up and putting their arms around our shoulders in very comradely fashion. In this way I got to know an army man quite well. He spoke good English and we would buy each other drinks throughout the days and talk about Russia and about other countries and sometimes he would play the piano and sing.

One of the waitresses who served us at this time was a statuesque blonde. She was about six feet two inches and very shapely and my eyes would follow her everywhere she went. My Russian friend, who seemed to know her well, noticed my interest and one day he said to me : 'You like?' 'Yes,' I said, 'I like.' We didn't speak again until she brought drinks to our table and he spoke to her in Russian. She looked at me and smiled and he said : 'Go with her.'

I stood up, not quite sure what was going on and she led me into one of the cubicles and pulled the curtains behind us. She started stripping off her clothes and I followed her cue. The cubicle wasn't the ideal place for sex. There was a table in the middle with two hard, narrow benches on either side and the flimsy curtain separating us from the rest of the company. But with that splendid body revealed, the difficulties seemed to evaporate and we made it on the table as if it were the finest fourposter bed in the world. The girl spoke no English at all, although her body spoke volumes, and I had no idea what to say after it was over. But she saved me any embarrassment by putting on her clothes and disappearing before I'd really caught my breath. I had no opportunity to give her any money and by the time I emerged from the cubicle she was back serving drinks at the tables. I don't think she was a real prostitute. When I rejoined my Russian friend he was very happy, as if he'd done something really great for me—which he had.

On a more mundane level, I remember we discussed the economic details of our lives and he was horrified to hear of the seven guineas a week rent I had to pay out of a basic salary of about £55 a month. He couldn't understand how I could manage on it and he explained to me how Russian workers in state-owned houses paid a rental of one or two roubles a month—7s to 10s as it then was. It was clear that although he might not have had a big choice of things to spend his money on, he did have more money to spend on what there was than his English equivalent.

In all I went backwards and forwards to Russia for about seven months and finally got back a day late for the birth of my daughter. I had got hung up on Russian names and we called her Alicia Gruschenka.

I'd managed to replenish our capital a bit with my seaman's pay and, due to the baby, I didn't go back to sea again immediately. Instead I hung around not knowing quite what to do with myself. Inevitably I started to haunt my old gaming houses —the only places where I had any social contacts to help me pass the time.

This rather negative existence dragged on for about eighteen months before I hauled myself up in another desperate attempt to go straight. I signed on with another Swedish vessel going to North Africa.

The depths of my discontent may be gauged by the fact that, at the age of twenty-eight or twenty-nine, and having achieved the dizzy heights of chief petty officer in my past career, I now took a job as a deck boy. I arrived at Sittingbourne in Kent in my sharp-looking suit to join the vessel only to be told that the job I'd been sent for was gone and the only vacancy was for a boy to swab down the decks. I pictured the soulless round back in Notting Hill and anything at all seemed preferable. You can't be serious, the captain said when I told him I'd take the job. I bought myself a pair of dungarees to show I was.

My promotion was pretty rapid as we went back and forth: junior ordinary seaman in Sweden, ordinary seaman in Guadeloupe, able seaman in the Mediterranean. The skipper saw that I filled the vacancies as they arose.

After ten months of this, I came off the boat to go to gaol. I had survived attempts to put me away for robbery with violence and running a brothel; I foundered on the theft of a few tins of paint.

Paint is brought onto ships in quantities of 200-300 cans at a time. There's always a lot of it lying about apparently spare—and everybody takes it. This would be considered about on a par with using the office stationery for private correspondence. I was using it to decorate my flat between trips, and nobody was missing it. Except some landlubber of a watchman on the docks. He came aboard eventually to report that I was leaving the ship with the cans. He was probably looking for a free drink.

I'm pretty sure nobody on the ship would have cared about the loss of a bit of paint. Even the skipper would have turned a blind eye. But the watchman, by reporting it, forced their hand. There was an investigation and I was arrested, tried and sent to gaol for three months.

Canterbury Gaol was cleaner than Brixton, at least, and I was put on sewing mailbags, which isn't much different from sewing canvas on a ship. Home from home.

After a few days I was transferred to an open prison at East-church, a sort of rehabilitation centre from which they're supposed to find you work when you're discharged. Most prisoners were doing farm work, but I didn't fancy that and they put me in a metal yard, salvaging metal. This was no drudgery for me. In the years I'd worked on ships one of the things I'd liked most was using my hands—for splicing wire and ropes, making mats and things like that. In the metal yard I worked at a bench re-covering metal from old telephone cables, splitting them down and extracting and separating the various metals. I would find myself doing more than the others, which made the prison officer happy.

The three months soon went. So did my marriage.

I had one visit every four weeks from Desirée and our relationship deteriorated completely. I told her I was going back to hustling when I got out and she wouldn't have any part of it, saying she didn't want to have me spending the rest of my life in gaol. There was little capital left and we were getting on each other's nerves. There were other differences, too, but some things are better left unsaid. . . . In short, we decided to part company.

The prison officer had promised to help me get a job and when I left, he recommended me to a metal yard in Kentish Town. I was given work there and expected to be doing something at least as interesting as I had been doing in prison. But, in fact, my job consisted of feeding iron from old cars and bedsteads into a massive, clanging machine which cut it into lengths. The pay was poor, too, and after a few weeks I simply couldn't stomach the job any more. The work scene had become something I couldn't take and hustling seemed the answer to everything.

I had found myself a flat in Notting Hill and I decided to go into hustling seriously. I turned a room into a shebeen and in no time I had made enough money to put a deposit on a house in Islington, have it redecorated and move my family in. Desirée had been working as a maid to make ends meet, but now she was able to quit the job and look after the children properly. Sometimes I would arrive at the house to see my daughters and take them out, but on the whole, I devoted myself to making money. I succeeded and began to buy a few leases on places here and there and re-let them. Money made more money and I opened another basement gaming house—the most elaborate that Notting Hill had known.

The basement was large—unlike the usual poky little places —and I had it nicely decorated with white walls, green carpets, luxury fittings and installed a man at the door to usher the guests discreetly in. My winning gimmick was to employ a couple of attractive French girls to serve free tea, coffee and sandwiches to the gamblers. The cost of the service was negligible compared with the clients' spending, but it stamped a special quality on the house and captivated every gambler in Notting Hill.

I had no interest in gambling myself, since gamblers hardly ever win—only the house. But some days I would pay an assistant to play with me. We would play for high stakes, £10-£20 a time, and since nobody knew he was a 'shill'—working for me—our game would create a lot of excitement and gamblers would be going out to gather more money so that they could win the sort of amount they saw changing hands. Occasionally I would join a table with the notion of losing £5 or so just to keep business ticking over and I invariably seemed to win, which was very disruptive for my discipline.

I had three full-time staff running the games and I discouraged them from gambling altogether. I liked the idea of my staff being completely satisfied and feeling they were being taken care of. I took them to a bank, opened accounts for them and taught them how to save money. If they wanted to gamble, I would tell them that they mustn't get involved in the games. I couldn't see anyone who was involved giving an impartial decision and I wanted my clients to know that there was no cheating. I was so strong about this that one day when I found one of my staff looking very sad and he said he'd got involved in a dice game and lost £120 I gave him the sack on the spot. He immediately became my enemy, but the lesson was probably a good one in the long run, because he works like mad for my organisation now and is doubtless a wiser man.

The gaming house led to yet another business. A gambler gets very involved and, if he's losing money, will take off his watch or his ring and ask you to hold it and lend him £5. So I took another room in the house and set up as illicit pawnbroker. I had boxes full of watches, chains, rings and all sorts of jewellery in no time, while the owners ploughed the money back into my gaming house. It was all very lucrative.

Thus I found myself in the centre of a small, successful empire of shebeen, gaming house, pawnshop, property renting. It involved quite a bit of organisation and this experience produced in me an unexpected ambition—to run a legitimate business.

14

The business I had in mind was a record shop. People were always buying records; people were always making them. It seemed like a good thing to be in. Admittedly it might have got no further than my mind but for the fact that a young Englishman came into partnership with me. His name was John and he was a man after my own heart.

I had first met him when I was selling the house in Colville Terrace. He came with his partner to look it over and see if it was worth adding to their property holdings. They were both very good-looking, personable young men and there the similarity ended. John's partner was the snappily-dressed, sharp, efficient businessman. John was the one with the inherited money and the interest in people rather than deals. He was decadently, sloppily dressed, with unpressed pants and a jacket that looked like his grandfather's and probably was. Once inside the house he seemed to forget what he'd come for immediately he saw some paintings of mine on the walls—and we plunged into a discussion on art while his partner surveyed the amenities.

Painting had filled my spare moments on board ship throughout the years. I had produced my abstracts and surrealist portraits on scraps of canvas torn from hatches which were being converted to metal. Usually I would give them away, or leave them here and there with friends. Once I got settled I collected a few back to adorn the walls.

John painted, too—pop art. He liked my work very much.

During the whole time I knew him, the only thing he ever tried to pressure me about was to carry on painting.

When he decided to buy the property and asked me around to his office a few days later to discuss details, I had the distinct impression the only things he really wanted to discuss were the pre-Raphaelites and the post-Impressionists. In fact, we talked about everything under the sun over a late breakfast of kippers in a nearby Lyons.

I really enjoyed his company and since it took me nearly a month to move after selling the house, we began to see a lot of each other. He was the sort of person who was as much at home in a shebeen as a West End club and he knew people everywhere. He had an unquenchable appetite for getting to know about everyone and everything—without getting too deeply involved himself. He was a very different type of Englishman from those I'd met in the past : not in the least condescending, or coming on as if he wanted to do things for you when he really didn't. He was a very happy-go-lucky fellow. I soon discovered, too, that he had that quality of genuine eccentricity that some English have like no other nationality.

I remember he once rather shocked me by announcing that he was going to take part in a Fascist Party demonstration. I found this so astonishing that I went along to Oxford Street to see it with my own eyes. There were masses of people around and a protective string of policemen. Violence, as usual, was expected from the presence of this anti-black, anti-Jewish rally. The crowds had that strained, wound-up look as if they would erupt at any moment. The Fascist procession swung in sight and the eruption, when it came, was one of laughter.

There was John, prominently displayed, marching merrily along with a beautiful black lady on each arm. It was his way of showing his contempt. As a scene it really knocked me out.

When I moved to Stoke Newington John made the long journey to visit me there every so often. I would return from hustling and find him sitting with Desirée, chatting, or playing with the children. Sometimes I would return the compliment and visit him in his house in Pimlico.

He lived in it alone amidst a strange assortment of antique gramophones, old furniture and stuffed birds. It was a very homely confusion and the token payment to modernity, the telephone, was all broken up on the floor and you had to kneel down and put the pieces together if you wanted to talk.

One day John came to see my gaming house and was most amused by it. I told him about my ambition to go into some legitimate business and he got quite enthusiastic about the idea. He suggested that second-hand books should be sold with the records and we began to discuss ideas. We ended that day deciding to run a business as equal partners. A few days later we picked premises in the better part of Islington, had them altered and decorated and installed a manager and his family in the flat above.

Looking back, I can see the business was doomed from the start. It was just a way of having fun. In the first place, John always treated money with a great amount of indifference and didn't bother to concern himself with the details of any venture. And I suppose I am rather similar. I've often been eager to make money, but it's always gone as easily as it's come. I've hardly ever had a weekly wage and I've never been a hoarder.

In the second place, we didn't bother to consider for a moment the requirements of the area when stocking up; we simply catered for our own tastes. And in the third, we found an insurmountable obstacle to our frequent meetings for business discussions in the form of the pub across the street, where we would expound about art and literature and life, but never, somehow, about business.

Not that we were lacking in theory. It was the practical details we found a little unmanageable.

One theory we developed, for instance, was about space saving. We reckoned the reason the small shopkeeper was on the way out was because he didn't know how to use space. We weren't going to fall into that trap and we erected little partitions inside the premises to divide it into record shop, bookshop and coffee bar. The coffee bar was something that just happened. We probably thought it would provide us with an alternative to the pub. In fact, it was a white elephant. We couldn't find any staff to run it and decided to sell the space to Fortes. They kept sending people to have a look at it, but there was always some further point they wanted to discuss and the space began to look more and more forlorn beside the busily brimming stocks of records and books next door. Eventually we let it to a Spanish lady, who knew as much about running a coffee bar as we did about running a record shop. She got further and further in arrears with the rent and neither of us had the heart to be hard with her. Finally, when she did a moonlight flit, we decided to throw in the tea-towel over the coffee bar.

Neither the record shop nor the bookshop were doing very well either. The main reason was they just weren't a good combination. Records have a new look, second-hand books an old one. We began to take the books home to read, until our places looked like public libraries. At that point we decided to replace them in the shop with paperbacks.

Business still didn't improve, however, and we became convinced that the only way we were going to make it was by expanding. We needed a second shop so that we could spin the stock around between them. This meant throwing good money after bad, which we obviously had reservations about. But as things turned out, the money was provided for us.

Around this time, friends invited us to a Sunday evening small rave scene in Hampstead. It was a party given by two girls, a twenty-one-year-old English heiress and a wealthy American of partly coloured extraction.

John and I arrived at their house and were ushered into the room where the party was going on. It was a one-woman show. A nondescript crowd of hangers-on—the types who are always waiting for handouts and free marijuana and drink—were sprawled all over the floor and the American girl was dancing, which was a complete theatrical performance. She was very beautiful and sexy—like an old-time vamp, but with this hint of colour. She had once danced in West Side Story and although she'd left the musical she'd never stopped dancing it. She would dance it all day, in fact, with an audience or without. If a few mirrors were around so that she could see herself in action, so much the better.

We sat down on the thick carpet to watch her. Were drawn down, rather, since the carpet was heated like an electric blanket and to stretch out on it was a sensual experience. Once down there, the only thing that stood out in the room was this girl, Maria. It was like being in a cinema, watching the star in a film.

She had long black hair pulled back from a face of classical proportions. A lemon-green shirt was tied tight around her breasts over a bare midriff and her sexy hips, which gyrated constantly in time with the music from the record player, were sheathed in skin-fitting purple tights. Rave scene it was.

The English girl, Angela, was that large, tennis-playing type who can either look incredibly scruffy, or can do herself up to look like some elegant English rose. She was usually quite content to run around in dungarees and a jersey. Dressed like that she would spend her time being the hostess or setting the stage for the parties which she and Maria gave.

There was plenty to drink and smoke at the party and, after a while, when we'd had a surfeit of looking at those hips, John and I began to move around, glancing at books—many of which were first editions—pouring a drink, digging the scene.

It soon became obvious that Maria was dancing for me. Wherever I went she was there, revolving her hips at me, reaching out with her arms, withdrawing, coming back again. She seemed to be saying : 'Look, but don't touch.'

In the meantime John got talking to Angela. They came from the same type of background and clearly she felt a strong affinity to him immediately, in contrast to the drags who normally surrounded her. I joined them later. And Maria joined us. So there we were : a nice little foursome.

Both girls were bored, restless, out for kicks. That was enough for them to be interested in us and on top of that neither of us was the type of man who immediately tries to make every girl he claps eyes on, which doubtless made us just that bit more intriguing. We spent about five hours at the party and from then on we began to visit the girls regularly. In fact you could almost say the party just went on.

Inevitably we talked about what we wanted to do with ourselves. Angela told us how she was interested in dress designing and had plans for putting on a big dress show with Maria. John and I talked about our interest in small businesses and our theory of space saving. We'd already spent so much time talking about it to each other that I suppose we sounded like knowledgeable businessmen. We did to Angela, at least. She suddenly asked if she could come in with us on our expansion plans. It would be fun, she said and she was sure the returns on her money would be higher than they were with her present investments. We asked her how much she was thinking of investing and she replied : 'How much do you need?'

John and I had been talking of buying a house in Notting

Hill to convert into a second shop and we worked out on paper how much we would need for a deposit and rebuilding. Angela glanced at the figure, promptly wrote out a cheque and gave it to us. Nobody was giving her a hard sell; she just handed us the money.

So we paid the deposit on a place and started having it renovated, fitting the basement out as a sort of little factory where she could carry on her dress business.

When it came to stocking out the various shops we established in these new premises, we discussed the money required and came up with a figure of £4,000. We never got as far as dividing it up. Angela simply asked Maria to pass her handbag and signed another cheque on the spot. That was the pattern from then on We only had to mention money and she'd say : 'Here it is.'

Angela liked John, and Maria, who would normally advise her and stop her throwing her money about, had this great desire for me and consequently was prepared to go along with the whole thing. I don't know why Maria got so bitten, though she did once say that she didn't like men touching her and they were always trying to do just that. I wasn't eager to touch her at all; she was too good to look at from a distance. I wasn't playing a game, but my indifference to her in that way made her that much more interested in me. She even got to showering me with presents : gold cuff links, half a dozen cashmere sweaters at a time, a dozen shirts. There were no half measures about Maria.

While we were getting things going, we tried to have a series of business discussions and were even less successful as a quartet than John and I had been as a couple. We would decide on a date, make all the necessary phone calls and arrange a meeting place. Having met, we would immediately take off on our favourite diversion. John's choice was always the pie stall outside the Houses of Parliament; Maria liked to go and drink in a certain pub in Windsor; Angela's thing was to drive to Cambridge and go boating on the river; my kick was a shebeen in the ghetto. Business never managed to rear its ugly head.

I found myself very easily caught up in the activities of the two girls. Life was a never-ending party. We put deposits on two more properties in Islington; I acquired a red Thunderbird as a flag to wave through Notting Hill; anything we wanted was ours—a shop, a house . . . like so many ice cream cones. We were all infused with the same spirit. I remember one day we went walking, looking for furs to put in the dress show, which was now being planned. Maria tried on a chinchilla in a shop, turning this way and that, looking at herself. 'Would you like it?' I asked. 'Yes.' I bought it on the spot. If you're at a party and someone asks for a drink, you don't have to think about it, you give him one. She wanted a chinchilla and she should have it. Even the first sex between us was like a party.

The forthcoming dress show began to take on flesh. Literally. Angela engaged a whole host of professional coloured models at top prices. They were to show off the clothes while dancing to pop music. It was all very exotic. Maria spent her time teaching the models to dance to West Side Story. She was in her element and, since she needed more room to move them around, Angela hired a hall for dress rehearsals. John and I left our shops in the charge of the managers and settled down to enjoy this new scene. We had our duties. I would time Maria with a stop watch while she danced from one end of the hall to the other; John would ferry drinks up and down. It was much more entertaining than books and records. Angela sat with us watching and sketching and getting more and more jittery as the great day approached.

This was to be the first presentation of clothes to pop music in London. In fact, Angela and Maria started this whole swinging London scene as far as clothes were concerned. Mary Quant, who had only just started, was square in comparison. The models modelled in bare feet; the skirts were very much mini; built-in jacket and trouser suits were one of the highlights. It was quite revolutionary.

With a few days to go, Angela appeared to be ready to break into little pieces. The day before the show she collapsed with a high fever. We had hired the huge ballroom of one of London's biggest hotels, invited just about everyone and now there was nobody really capable of handling the show from the business side. However, the show must go on, so we hired a suite of rooms way up in the hotel for Angela and had closed-circuit television installed so that she could watch the show from her bed.

The whole world seemed to turn up : lords, ladies, debs, poets, painters, press and quite a few black faces I'd brought in. There was a West Indian band I'd turned on to play the sort of music I knew would keep everybody happy. In no time the place was full, the food and drink overflowing, the models dancing West

Side Story to perfection under Maria's expert eye. It was a ball.

But as business, the show was a complete failure, a complete turn on and off. People liked the clothes and were eager to buy, but when they tried to talk business, they couldn't find anyone to talk to. Angela was absent. John and I didn't know enough about it. And Maria, who was only interested in the artistic side and how her models were dancing, was rude to everyone. She loved the clothes and didn't really want to sell any of them.

I remember at one point a wealthy young deb who was renowned for the sums she spent on clothes was admiring a suede and leather dress and wanted to buy it. She eventually found Maria and asked how much it would be. Maria looked down her nose and said, icily : 'Why—do *you* want to buy it?'

Not a single thing was sold.

We all repaired to the suite when the show was over and tried to console Angela who was very depressed about the lack of sales. She and Maria wanted something to take them out of themselves, new people to talk to, so I ordered a few cars and went to my old haunts in Notting Hill to round up some of my old cronies.

A new happening began. The hotel suite filled up with pot-smoking West Indians and by night John's Chelsea friends had turned up. That's how a two-day party got under way. We hired Don Brown and his jazz band and Ronnie Scott. We had room service going so that a constant procession of liquor and appetising dishes kept arriving to accompany the pot and the music.

The girls were delighted; some of my cronies out of their depth.

West Indians are not very adventurous with their palates, peas and rice being the order of the day. Finding themselves turned loose in a luxury hotel with a yard-long menu in French and smart waiters saying 'yes sir', 'no sir', to their every whim, completely knocked them out. The waiters were in their element with lordly interpretations of the menu and I'd hear people saying : 'Can we really have *anything*? Anything we want?' And they'd end up ordering every single item to make sure they didn't miss anything worth having. Sometimes the sophistication of the menu nearly created a riot. One waiter asked a big Jamaican named Ivan if he wanted snails. Ivan hauled his huge frame slowly from his chair, glowering, and lunged at the man with a mighty clenched fist. A whole mass of people rushed between them and while John slipped the cowering waiter a fiver to smooth things over, Ivan was herded back to his chair snarling: 'Think I'm a fucking savage!'

Throughout the two days several hundred people passed through the party. A beatnik arrived from Tangier with a sackful of pot and became the resident pusher; the aristocracy kept appearing and going discreetly wild. It baffles me how we all escaped being put in gaol. There was so much noise that guests from other parts of the hotel were constantly hammering on the door to complain. Guys would be standing there apoplectic in their pyjamas and then when we opened the door and they saw all the drinks and ladies and fun and games, they'd go straight off and change into a suit to come and join us. Quite a few of the West Indians changed out of their suits when they discovered they could get them pressed by room service. They'd be running around in their underpants in the pot smoke, adding to the local colour.

Angela and Maria loved it. They were on the telephone calling people they knew in Rome and Boston, telling them to come on over because there was a rave party going on. And their erratic friends from those places were actually coming—haring straight in from the airport by hired car.

Once or twice the press dropped in, trying to get interviews to do with the dress show, which now seemed something of the distant past. They'd find everyone stoned and either give up or join in.

John eventually developed this paranoia about everybody getting busted and was trying to avert it by distributing fivers amongst the waiters, who were being tipped very lavishly all round. The hotel management must have had some anxious moments, but they dug the publicity, with people being telephoned to come from the other side of the world. And they couldn't very well put us out with the bill growing to astronomical proportions.

I was particularly impressed by the way everyone got on so well. Problems of colour didn't enter into the situation. But then the upper classes don't have that problem in England; nothing really touches them. The only condescension from white to black. during that week came from the hotel employees, not the guests.

All in all the round-the-clock fun and games were pretty wearing. Personally, I almost died and had to take off to Majorca to recuperate in a quiet house lent me by a friend. Angela went off to the country to recover in the bosom of her family and Maria set herself up in Chelsea, failed to persuade me to join her, got bored and eventually danced out of the country to the phantom strains of West Side Story.

While I was away, John and Angela decided, as principal partners, to put the company we'd formed to run our various businesses into voluntary liquidation. By the time I returned it didn't exist any more. Any capital that could be realised was returned to Angela and everything else was allowed to die a natural death. The bookshops and record shops ground to a halt as the stock ran out; houses were lost because nobody took up the options on the deposits. I was left with a red Thunderbird and my basement gaming house in Notting Hill. End of another attempt to go straight.

15

Not unnaturally, I found it hard to settle back into the ghetto life and I left the gaming house staffed by a couple of managers and began to spend time with my children.

They loved the Thunderbird and I started getting a lot of fun out of driving them all over the place, in and out of London, buying them clothes and toys and enjoying their company. When I saw Desirée, too, the strained relations between us seemed to have eased a little with time and I was able to talk to her a bit, and listen.

Looking back, this period was something of a crossroads in my life. I was racing around not having much idea of where I was going and what I wanted out of life. And then I met Nancy and everything began to change.

Nancy was introduced to me at a friend's house. I looked at this strikingly attractive Canadian-Jewish girl and a vivacious intelligence shone out of her eyes and dazzled me. She had beautiful short red hair, which I thought would look fabulous if it were long, and she had her legs crossed to reveal a hole in the top of her stocking, which I found a delightfully kinky thing. She was a journalist and, as such, very interested in knowing about what was happening in London—particularly among the immigrants. She asked so many questions about the ghettoes that I offered to show her around. She thought that would be a nice idea and we began to see a lot of each other. Sometimes when she went to some other part of the country on a job I would go with her, maybe taking one of my daughters along.

I found Nancy very good company. She could be very tense and clam up every so often, as if she were afraid to talk or do anything. And then she could let herself go and be relaxed and gay and amusing, when she was so nice to look at and be with that I wanted her to be like that all the time. She was a very sympathetic listener to everything I cared to tell her about— the past, what I liked doing, what I planned to do—which was precious little, if I remember.

Talking with Nancy, a slow transformation began in me. She made me think more deeply—really think, about broader issues than those concerning immediate survival. She encouraged me to read and gave me books. I had spent a lot of time reading on board ship, mostly novels of the Somerset Maugham type. Now I began to read more purposefully and with greater awareness, devouring people like James Baldwin, Colin MacInnes and Norman Mailer, whose 'White Negro' knocked me out. I developed a great thirst for knowledge.

We also spent a lot of time going to the theatre, which Nancy adored, and instead of hanging around shebeens, which had been my kick, we would go to dinner with friends of Nancy's and talk with them. *She* would talk with them. It was brought home to me how limited my vocabulary and general knowledge were. I had ideas, but they were superficial and my lack of background information about current affairs made my arguments very weak. Sometimes I wouldn't even know what they were talking about. Even when they discussed Trinidad I couldn't say much as I didn't know what was happening.

I had also never discussed with any serious person why people like me turned into hustlers, but now I began to take a look at myself and investigate my own circumstances and the reactions they produced. Even my appearance underwent a change for Nancy's sake. Since my poncing days I'd always worn several rings on my fingers—one of the hallmarks of the profession. Nancy thought this very vulgar and I cut them down to one. My clothes, too, became more conservative, lost their old flash. I was on my way to becoming respectable.

Eventually, Nancy and I took a holiday at my friend's house in Majorca and then went to live together in a flat in Primrose Hill.

I wanted to cut my ties with the ghetto again. It was a connection which seemed to blinker me so that I never saw the world outside. The gaming house, which continued to provide me with some money, was merely stumbling along in my absence. I no longer found it exciting or desirable to be there. Nancy was rather moralistic about hustling, just the way Desirée had been, and was constantly pressuring me to stop wasting my life running around in circles and do something worth while. The fact that both women had taken the same attitude made the effect on me all the stronger. I was terribly eager to please Nancy and so I decided to go to school and learn something about sociology, which was a subject I found increasingly interesting.

At this point I went to see Donald Chesworth and told him about my aims and I brought him to meet Nancy. During the course of this meeting, he offered to help get me enrolled at Ruskin College, Oxford, if I would first gain the required O levels at school. Nancy was enthusiastic about this plan and I enrolled at a college in Holborn and got busy on the usual range of subjects.

Life has seldom gone smoothly with me, however, and it wasn't going to start now. I had books to buy, fees to pay and, with the gaming house tottering, no money to operate with. I had other commitments, too : Desirée's upkeep and my own rent and living expenses. I just had to find money and the only way I knew was by hustling. The result was that I would miss one lecture because I was too busy, make myself very upset and swear it wouldn't happen again—and then miss another. There were only so many hours in a day and eventually I became thoroughly disheartened and gave up school altogether. I suppose I went to about twenty lessons in all.

Other things were happening, too. In my mind. Turmoil.

Since I'd started going out with my children again I'd begun to miss them a lot and want to be with them. Desirée had changed, too, now that she felt reasonably secure in the house in Islington. I found myself split in two. I wasn't sure whether I wanted to stay with Nancy or go back to Desirée. There was a terrible lot of indecision and I was quite tortured with not knowing what to do and consequently doing both very badly. From Nancy's point of view, our relationship had helped her to relax in some ways, but, by its very tenuous nature had produced other tensions in her. It was fortunate in a way that her job suddenly took her back to Canada for a few months. I was able to be alone and think about what I really wanted to do.

I kept the gaming house going, but I had no heart for it. I had so changed that I began to do really ridiculous things from a hustler's point of view: like bringing in billiards and table tennis so that clients spent more time playing for fun than gambling. Although I had no conscious wish to provide a purely social forum, I was subconsciously destroying my own gaming business.

It certainly provided no solution to my financial problems and, in desperation, I went to see John's partner.

I called on him just at the right time. He had just completed buying a whole street, Powis Terrace, in Notting Hill, and he had a load of problems managing it. This was the job he offered me at a respectable salary and I took it. There wasn't a lot of work involved. He was converting the houses into service flats and needed someone to supervise the charladies and let prospective tenants in to view. I had a nice office to work in and the boys from the area were able to come in and while away an hour or two chatting every day. Sometimes I could turn them on to odd jobs if they wanted them. And once they turned me on to something.

People are always buying and selling in the area and one of the most saleable commodities is marijuana. It seems an Indian from a ship in the docks had approached some hustlers with a whole sackful—about twenty pounds—for which he wanted immediate cash. They had neither the money nor the set-up to impress him and they came to me to see if I could use the office in some way to con it off him.

As far as I was concerned it was fun and games and I'd always enjoyed those. So he came to see me and there I was behind this huge desk on a fitted carpet with telephones buzzing importantly. I made sure I opened a drawer and gave him a glimpse of stacks of money, which were the rents and petty cash. He was visibly impressed that here was a flourishing business.

He offered me the pot at his price and I said it was too high. If I was going to buy that quantity, I wasn't going to pay that much. We haggled a bit and finally agreed on £55 per pound. Had the money been available, this would have been a worthwhile deal, anyway. If you sell it straight, by the ounce, the price is £8 per ounce, which would make the overall value of the pot £2,560. But on the retail market, you mix it with other herbs you can buy from a chemist and increase its quantity considerably. The price goes up the smaller the quantity you sell: half ounces, £1 parcels which will make four to five cigarettes, little joints at an individual price of 5s. There would be a mere fraction of a half ounce in the joint. The peddlers who roll joints and hand them out at all-night cafés all over London make phenomenal profits. But they tend to smoke a large part of these away themselves and by entertaining their friends with the stuff. They never seem to have the money to make big deals like this one.

The Indian was clearly happy at the outcome—which would bring in £1,100—and appeared convinced he'd found a good buyer. As for me, I hadn't the remotest idea how I was going to get the pot from him without paying for it. We hadn't been able to work out a plan; it was just a question of ad-libbing.

I let him toddle merrily away to collect the stuff and I sat there with my mind open, but empty.

Now it happened that during the morning there'd been a burglary in one of the flats and the police had been around investigating. They had to come back that afternoon for a bit more routine poking around and they chose the moment that my Indian friend came back to the office. He had just plonked the sack down on the desk when I saw the police car pull up in the street below and these policemen getting out. I looked at the Indian, who was rigid with terror, and I shouted : 'Run—run like hell!' I pointed to a window at the back of the office and he went through it like a performing dog through a hoop—and never once looked back.

I took the sack and put it in a cupboard. The police went about their business. And the Indian was never seen again.

I turned the pot over to friends who knew how to handle it and we made a small fortune. It was one of the very few times I was grateful to the forces of law and order.

With this little nest egg, I was able to give up work for a while and devote myself to reading and talking with friends. I had become more and more interested in learning of the history and views of various black peoples throughout the world and I was soaking up everything I could lay my hands on, from black nationalism to the writings of Mao Tse-tung.

Knowledge was giving me confidence and I would find myself entering into the arguments which constantly take place inside the gaming houses and barbers' shops in the area—those West Indian type political arguments that solve the problems of the world in five minutes flat.

It was in a barber's shop run by a Trinidadian named Nakki Blake that I first heard the name Malcolm X, which was to mean so much to me in the future. Nakki could solve almost any argument that broke out in his shop by quoting Malcolm X and he did so constantly with telling effect.

I was intrigued, naturally, by a black man with no surname who had an answer for everything, but the Moslem message didn't get across to me at that time. I read as much as I could about the Black Muslims in the Press, but they were presented more or less as a bunch of lunatics and, I must admit, their set-up didn't seem very realistic as viewed through this hostile presentation. Apart from this, although I had paid lip service to the idea of black organisations being wholly black, when it came to a hard realisation of what this really meant, I found myself quite lacking in confidence. This is the black man's burden. He was born with the idea that the white master takes care of him. In slavery, he remembers, the man who held the whip was a white man and, deep inside, he knows the white man is still the man with the gun. In short, he retains a considerable fear of the white man and doubts his own ability to manage for himself.

While Nancy was away, a close relative of hers who was in London at the time, invited me to have supper with him. I had met him a few times before when he came to the house to see her. He was not the sort of man I would make a bosom friend of, but he had always been very civil towards me and the relationship between us was quite cordial. So it seemed quite reasonable that he should invite me to supper and we went to a little restaurant in the West End. We chatted about countries he had visited and about a marvellous holiday he'd had in the West Indies while we ate. We were just about finishing the meal when he came out with the real purpose of his invitation. It was to tell me he didn't approve of my relationship with Nancy.

I gave him a sympathetic ear. Looking at it objectively I could see he would wish for something better for her. There I was, a hustler, a married man with three children, and there Nancy was, a member of the Winnipeg Jewish bourgeoisie. Clearly he had valid grounds for objection. But then he suddenly said: 'I must tell you quite plainly and truthfully that I could not take kindly to Nancy marrying a black man.'

I was astounded. He had all those valid objections to call on and instead he chose colour. And when I recovered from my astonishment, I figured he must be in a bad way and felt terribly sorry for him. His objection was pure white racism and I consider all racists to be sick and stupid people.

We separated outside the restaurant. There was no further discussion possible between us.

16

Nancy came back from Canada and we spent happy months in Primrose Hill just living, going to the theatre and the cinema, while I did the odd deal to make money.

Most of the time I felt as if I were in school although I'd formally given it up some time before. I was rabid to know what was happening in the world. I would have three newspapers a day now, having never bought one in my life before; every news on television I had to see; and, of course, I went on reading. I also began thinking again and finding some legitimate business to do.

Around that time I met a friend of Nancy's, visiting from Canada, who was in the clothing business. He was a big, very charming man who dressed well and never stopped talking about how much money he had and about his business, which turned out seven hundred suits a day. It seemed like a good industry to me and I was able to make a few contacts in the same field over here. I made them through a wheeler-dealer I knew from the Bahamas. He owned a hotel in London and was always buying and selling property, or building clubs and bars. At this time he was thinking of starting some small shops and had begun talks with some Jewish manufacturers from the East End about the possibility of his retailing a range of clothes they could produce cheaply. He knew I was interested in going into business and invited me to join in this deal. He and his Jewish friends were thinking only of selling in this country, but I began to consider the pros and cons of selling their goods abroad. I had Canada in mind for a strictly speculative venture. That way, I figured, I would not be tied down and stuck in an office. Movement was what I enjoyed and I could see myself acting as international middleman.

The concrete deal I came up with was to see who would be interested in a range of ties. They were very good and very cheap. At the same time, Nancy's father was having his sixtieth birthday, so I gave her a plane ticket to Winnipeg as a surprise and we took off together.

We had cabled Nancy's friend who owned the suit factory and he was at the airport to meet us with renewed invitations to stay at his place during our visit. He lived in a large and beautiful bungalow and he gave us a section of it. He was a generous host and we had a swinging time at his place. He lived with a coloured girl who was born in Canada and they had a nice relationship in which colour didn't seem to exist. The four of us would sit and chat during the day and go out to eat at a restaurant and see the town in the evening.

Nancy's parents pretended I didn't exist. She would spend some of the days with them and return to me in the evening. She went to her father's birthday party, but, of course, I wasn't invited. I must admit I was rather upset about it. I didn't see the need for the relationship to be that way. And in the middle of this I had a telephone call from her brother, who was also in Winnipeg at the time, to tell me he didn't think it would be a good idea for me to call at the house. I told him I could do without his advice and he said something to the effect that things were different here from London. . . . We had a rather nasty argument.

The result of this was that Nancy began to feel very strange about the whole thing and had some kind of talk with her mother after which she told me it would be a good idea, after all, if I met her parents. She added that the best time to see them was the weekend and that she had to leave for England before then because she had work to do. She was terribly nervous about the situation.

After Nancy had left, her mother phoned the house and we had a brief conversation in which we arranged a date and time for me to meet her.

At the specified time I arrived at the family home and viewed with some apprehension the big, part timbered, part concrete house with its huge bay windows. Nancy's father, who was a doctor, had his office in the basement and there was a stairway leading up the side of the building to the half-elevated first floor. I mounted this stairway and rang the bell. Nancy's mother opened the door to me. She was a good-looking woman, an older, smaller version of Nancy, and she was very polite, taking my coat, offering me a chair, being as civil as she would be to any stranger. I knew we were not going to be great friends, but I expected her to be very dignified about whatever it was she didn't like.

We had a little decorous small talk. I said what a beautiful house she had. She said they'd lived in Winnipeg a long time. I said it seemed an attractive city and I was enjoying my visit. She said her husband couldn't be there to meet me as he was in his surgery at the moment. She offered me a drink, which I declined, and coffee, which I accepted. And so we chatted in an aura of unreal calm until she suddenly blurted out: 'It's no use pretending. I don't believe in the relationship between you and Nancy.'

I said: 'So I understand, but I'm very happy with it and I rather think Nancy is, too. What more can anyone want?'

'My daughter is a very nervous child,' she said.

'I don't see what that's got to do with anything,' I said, 'and even if she was, she seems to have got over it now.'

'What do you intend to do?' her mother demanded and, before I had time to answer, launched into an emotional monologue on how she was always reading in the newspapers about the terrible things that happened to people in this inter-racial business and how she didn't want that for her daughter. She quoted something she'd read about racial trouble in Los Angeles and the store-looting going on there. I told her: 'That's the kind of world I live in.' I went on to admit I'd been a hustler in London for years and now I was in Winnipeg trying to do some straight business. Would she tell me what she was really objecting to—my mode of life? If that was the case, I figured I owed her a hearing.

She said no, it was not my mode of life she objected to, she simply didn't want her daughter being alienated from all her friends and having no social life. 'No neighbours will want to know you,' she cried, 'and you live in a slum—a cold water flat!'

I explained that by London standards the flat we lived in was rather elegant and comfortable. With geysers, I pointed out, cold water was the least of our problems. She insisted that a mixture of race could never work and I replied that I, personally, was very happy in it. At that she exploded, shouting: 'Of course you're happy, but my daughter isn't!' I said that if her daughter was unhappy, then I was unaware of it and, what was more, I didn't believe her daughter had told her she was unhappy. 'I am not holding her a prisoner,' I said. 'She's just been here and if she were unhappy and wanted to stay here she could.'

Her mother had been working herself gradually into a nervous state and suddenly she lost control completely and started screaming: 'If my daughter marries you, I'll jump through the window! I will—I'll jump through the window!'

I was terribly unnerved and distressed at this. It was more than I'd bargained for. I said as calmly as I could: 'Will you please sit down and try to calm yourself. Can I get you a glass of water?' But my words had no effect other than to goad her on in her screaming fit and she yelled: 'Don't touch me! Don't touch me!' I was nowhere near the woman and, at this, I began gathering my coat, saying that I was sorry to have upset her, but there was no point in my staying and I would go.

When I said this she made a big effort to pull herself together and said she would calm down and would I stay. I was rather confused, but I didn't feel able to leave with her asking me to wait and I sat down again.

After a few silent minutes, she said she knew it wasn't right for her to feel the way she did about coloured people. She waved her hand around the nicely furnished room and said her daughter grew up in this type of background and society and was entitled to money, comforts, social life and so on. I was well aware, listening to her, that she would like nothing better than for Nancy to marry a nice Jewish boy and settle in Winnipeg, but that wasn't the way things were. What could I do about that? I didn't comment. I just sat there feeling embarrassed.

Then she asked me outright: 'Will you leave my daughter alone?' There was just no answer to that. I wasn't molesting her in any way. How could I leave her? Her mother put the question again and I was forced to say: 'What you are asking is just not possible. It's perfectly obvious Nancy and I are very happy. I don't really feel, at this point, that there's anything you and I can usefully talk about.'

She took that without any reaction, as if she didn't hear it, and she began to tell me again about the trouble with black people all over the world—in America, Africa. In the middle of this, it suddenly seemed to hit her that it was black people she was talking about and she exploded again and began screaming all hell.

I couldn't take any more and I said I was leaving, picking up my coat for the second time. Again she made a big effort to control herself and blurted out : 'My sister would like to meet you. Will you stay and see her?' I said I couldn't see any point in it and she replied : 'I can't help myself. I would like my sister to talk to you. Will you please see her?'

I should have left, but I felt virtually a prisoner, as if I had to treat her like a sick person. What can you do with sick people like that? I wish I'd never seen it. But I decided to humour her and agreed to wait while she telephoned her sister to come over.

She offered me another coffee in the tense truce period while we waited. I was very hesitant, but I accepted, which I think was the bravest thing I did in Winnipeg.

Her sister arrived fairly soon and Nancy's mother met her with an agitated cry : 'This is the man!' From the way she said it I felt as if she saw me as some awful prehistoric monster and she followed it up with a confused version of what we'd been talking about, getting more and more upset as she went on. The sister kept quite calm, however, and I interrupted to explain that I'd been invited over and had come in good faith and was very sorry to see Nancy's mother in this state. This was too much for the mother and she began to cry : 'You tell him! You tell him! I've told him if Nancy marries him nobody will talk to her or have her in their house—and he doesn't believe me! You tell him!'

I looked at the sister, who said nothing and Nancy's mother cried : 'Would you have him in your house?'

The sister, who was much more restrained, was clearly embarrassed and she said : 'Look Becky, try to calm yourself.'

A little bit of the devil got in me then and I said to the sister : 'Yes—tell me, would you have me in your house?'

She parried that with a question of her own. 'Are you going to marry Nancy?' she asked.

I said we had never discussed it and Nancy's mother exploded. 'They haven't even discussed it!' she gasped. 'You heard what he said!'

I had begun by feeling that Nancy's mother was sick; now I began to think she was just an unpleasant person, prepared to embarrass anybody and try to ride roughshod over them : it didn't seem to matter to her. I told her I didn't think she should act in that way—and her reaction was to get on the phone and call another sister to come over. I in turn got on the phone and called my host to come and pick me up out of there. I was confused by a ridiculous situation, and becoming ridiculous myself.

Our reinforcements arrived almost together. The new sister looked me straight in the eye and said it was a lot of nonsense dragging her away from her house and children over something like this and she'd be pleased to have me for tea some time. My host, who is probably one of the richest Jewish textile men in Canada, found himself in an atmosphere of high tension and got involved in the argument, himself, in the few minutes he was there.

Having failed to get support from the second sister, Nancy's mother turned to him and cried: 'He won't leave my daughter alone!'

'What do you mean?' my host asked.

'I've been trying to tell him nobody will talk to her and she'll lose all her friends,' the mother screamed, 'but he just won't let her go. She has his ring on her finger, his chain around her neck!'

My host stared at her and then he said: 'Well I've been at their house in London and if anyone's holding on to anyone else, Nancy's holding on to him. He doesn't keep her prisoner.'

At this point there were sounds of the father coming up from down below to see what all the shouting was about. One of the sisters indicated it might be a good thing if we all left. We slipped out to the sound of the mother's voice crying: 'Don't let him in here. His heart can't take it.'

I left Canada a couple of days later with a new vision of white motherhood. I have had no further contact with the family. As far as I am concerned they just don't exist. I feel sorry for Nancy, but what can I do? I'm sure she feels sorry for me and my problems with my own mother. If her mother and father came to London tomorrow and wanted to see their daughter they'd be welcome. That's only human. But I wouldn't suffer the same scene again.

Does Nancy's mother represent the majority of white people? I refuse to look on her as an isolated case. Whatever she may be, she certainly isn't that.

17

The encounter with Nancy's mother was a traumatic experience for me. It completely threw me and made me consider this black-white thing more deeply than ever before. It was while I was in this depressed state that I met Malcolm X for the first time.

I had returned to London without doing any business. I had no energy and couldn't decide about anything in the future at all. Nancy, who had returned to England before me, felt rather guilty, as if she'd deserted me in the line of fire. She exuded quiet sympathy, being very housewifely and pleasant, making all my favourite dishes and things like that. We didn't talk about her mother at all until letters started arriving from aunts some weeks later—and even then we said very little about the whole business.

The rent for my gaming house was paid up for a year, but I had closed down the gambling side completely and people simply went in to have free use of the table tennis, billiards and other sports facilities. There was no money from it and none from anywhere else. My efforts to go straight were still not meeting with any resounding success, but I couldn't go back to hustling. In fact, I couldn't go into Notting Hill. Instead I began frequenting a new scene, looking for something intangible. I started visiting all the centres where black people congregated: the West Indian Community Centre, the Congress of African Unity headquarters, all sorts of places where one could eat African food, browse in the libraries and talk to people in the discussion rooms. It was at the CAU headquarters in Earl's Court that I met Malcolm.

A West Indian friend and I had gone there to eat and Malcolm came in with the president of the Congress and a number of admirers and sat down at an adjacent table. I knew him only from the enthusiastic comments of Nakki Blake, the barber, and from pictures in the press. But when my friend pointed him out to me he seemed very familiar. I saw this tall, good-looking, light-coloured black man with his little goatee beard, his fur hat, his dark suit which achieved the impossible feat of appearing two sizes too big and still looking elegant, and it was exactly how I'd expected him to look.

He was on his way back to the United States after his second tour of Africa and he looked rather tired and withdrawn. I stared across the tables at this guy who was saying new and interesting things about the black man and telling him to be proud he was black and, with the impact of my experience in Canada still very much with me, I felt eager to talk to him, quietly and privately.

I wrote a brief note telling him this and giving my address and telephone number and then I went across to his table and introduced myself. He reacted with quiet courtesy and we talked for a few minutes. I asked him if he'd enjoyed his stay in Africa and how long he would be staying in Britain and where he would be speaking as I'd like to hear him. He said he had learned a lot from Africa, that he'd be staying some days in this country and that his first scheduled speech was at the London School of Economics. It was the customary small talk between strangers and it ended with my saying I'd like to talk to him at some point when he wasn't too busy, and would he call me. He said he would and as we shook hands I gave him the note, which he slipped in his pocket.

When I got home that afternoon I told Nancy that Malcolm X would be round that evening. I felt quite sure he would come. Nancy was rather worried as she understood he was a terrible racist, but I said I didn't intend to hide her and, in fact, would like her to meet him. Later that day I went to a film and when I returned home I found Malcolm had already 'phoned and said he'd call me again at 9.30 p.m. He did so on the dot and told me he was very tied up and asked if it would be convenient for him to come to my place an hour later.

He came by taxi and slipped quietly into the flat. I never knew him to make a grand entrance anywhere. He was very informal and completely lacking in social pomposity. He would walk into a room as he did that night and he was simply there—a part of the scene.

I introduced him to Nancy and he seemed a little nervous of her, a little apprehensive. We had a certain amount of small talk and he told us a bit about the Organisation of Afro-American Unity he was setting up in the United States—a militant black nationalist organisation prepared to defend itself against white supremacists in its search for human rights.

He had been working very hard and he was tired and tense. It turned out that he had a terrible headache and Nancy offered him a pill. I remember he looked at her very suspiciously and refused to take it. There was no doubt in my mind or hers that he wasn't prepared to take anything like that from a white woman.

I suggested we listen to some music for a while and he said that would be nice. He was particularly fond of Aretha Franklin and I had some records of hers which I played. She has a beautiful voice and the numbers she sang were soft and bluesy. They seemed to relax him a lot and we chatted some more and he suddenly said to Nancy : 'Perhaps I will have that pill.'

Nancy glanced at me and smiled. His change of mind was like a landmark. From then on he seemed to relax more and more and appeared to be happy with us. We talked and listened to music until one o'clock in the morning, and then he said he must be leaving and would I see him next day. I was pleased he wanted to see me and I said I would come to hear him speak at the LSE and meet him there. We had trouble calling a cab for him and eventually drove him back to his hotel ourselves.

Malcolm and I were already good friends by the time we dropped him that night. That's the way it happens with me. I can make friends very quickly, or not at all, and I think Malcolm was rather similar.

Nancy liked him, too. He turned out to be so unlike the image she'd had of him. Instead of this vaunted hatred of white people, he'd shown friendliness towards her and had been happy to include her in the conversation and answer her questions about America, his travels, his wife and children.

I turned up at the LSE next day and listened to him speak. The biggest hall in the place was packed with students wanting to hear him and he spoke to them quietly and authoritatively on Islam, his travels in Africa and the Middle East and on the black man in America. His basic theme, as always, was the injustice suffered by the black man, the violence done to him and the indignant outcry when he retaliated.

Malcolm really swung with those students, as I gathered he did with students in the States. He had a wonderful relationship with them simply because he told the truth, as he always did. Youth is always willing to accept the truth, hard though it may be sometimes. It was the students' parents who were terrified of Malcolm—simply because they were terrified of the truth. They were afraid it was going to threaten their existence—which it does, because they live a lie.

On that day, Malcolm completely captivated his audience; so much so, that when it came to question time nobody challenged anything he'd said. They simply asked him about his future plans.

I was terribly impressed with his technique, which was based on exhaustive research. He was a man with a fantastic wealth of information and he never went anywhere without his little black case which was a mobile library of statistics, ranging from the transportation of slaves hundreds of years ago to the latest figures on black poverty and things like that in America today. When Malcolm made a point there was really no possibility of argument. I still think he's the best speaker I've ever heard. The greatest compliment I ever had was when I subsequently spoke at Oxford and someone told me it was the best speech they'd heard since Malcolm X.

At the end of his talk, Malcolm was so surrounded by people —as he always was, although he seemed such a lonely figure— that I didn't try to get to him. I just went home and waited for him to call. When he did a little later, he said: 'I wanted to see you. Why didn't you wait?' I told him I'd thought he was too busy and he said he'd like to come around later, so we arranged for him to come to the flat at ten.

The quality which made Malcolm so human was a certain naïve boyishness which softened his preoccupation with his mission to better the black man's lot. We had an example of it that night when he rang me early in the evening to say his doctor had told him to go to bed with a brandy because he wasn't feeling too well. He paused as if he expected my judgement on this and

I said : 'Okay—you'd better do what the doctor tells you.' There was another pause and then he said : 'I'll think about it. I may still come up and see you.' He rang again an hour later to say : 'I'm going to take the brandy.' 'Go ahead,' I said. 'It'll do you good.' He rang off and the next call some time later was to say he was coming up.

He arrived with the coy smile of someone who's done something he considers a little eccentric and his first words were : 'I had the brandy, you know.' It must have been the first time he'd touched alcohol for very many years.

He revealed this quality in taxis, too. He would never discuss anything, because the taxi driver could overhear. If I ever started to talk, Malcolm would make a sign to me to indicate—'Cool it; there are enemies everywhere.' Although he listened to other people's comments and answered their questions, Malcolm did tend to make speeches all the time and was very much in command of the situation. He might have been a little wearing at times without his little-boy side.

That second night we sat and talked for a while and then Nancy and I took him for a drive around London. He wasn't interested at all in the usual touristic stuff. He wanted to see the areas where black people lived, so after pointing out Nakki Blake's barber's shop in Maida Vale where I'd first heard of him, I took him to Notting Hill and the other ghettoes. He was still talking quite a lot about his Organisation of Afro-American Unity and he suddenly asked me : 'What are you guys doing in England? And what do you aim to do in the future?' And then he looked me in the eye and added : 'What are *you* going to do?'

I said I didn't really know and pointed out that he wasn't familiar with how the black people were in England. They were very different from their counterparts in America, I said. They were very individualistic, all wanting to be leaders, very difficult to organise. But then, I admitted, I couldn't say I knew my own people very well.

Malcolm continued to look me in the eye and he said : 'Brother, I will give you your first lesson in leadership : the head can never tell the feet they are going the wrong way.'

This maxim of his stuck in my mind and although I tried desperately to work out what he really meant by it, the full significance didn't come to me until a long time afterwards when I was directing my own field workers. I was attempting to tell them they were going about things the wrong way and at that moment I realised that they were not wrong—I was. It was I who had to read more, learn more, in order to direct them better. Today I am a far more tolerant person than I was, thanks to that one sentence of Malcolm's.

The next day Malcolm was due to go to Birmingham to talk to the Islamic student body and I asked if I could go with him. 'Would you really come?' he asked. 'I'd be very happy to,' I said.

He got on the phone straight away to Birmingham and told the student organisation to book two rooms at his hotel. 'I'll be coming up with my brother—Brother Michael,' he said.

The Islam student body probably interpreted what he said literally. They booked me in at the Grand Hotel as Michael X—and that was how Michael X came into being. I was not a 'Black Muslim'. The X was a mistake. When I eventually did become a Moslem, I chose a different name, but the mistake went on.

We travelled to Birmingham by train. It was a remarkable thing about Malcolm that whatever he happened to be doing at any time, he could and would always relate it to his purpose. If he was listening to music, he would relate it to the creative energy of the black people and talk about that. Travelling in the train prompted him to get onto the subject of communications and he expatiated on the absolute necessity of building an effective communications network amongst our people. By this time it was already in our minds that I would help him set up a branch of his organisation in Britain and we talked a little about that, too.

We were met at Birmingham by a reception committee of Moslem students, who escorted us to the hotel, where I discovered my new name. Malcolm had a press conference in the evening before he was due to talk and somebody from the *Sunday Times* was trying to get through to him before it started. But, as usual, Malcolm's phone was constantly busy and the hotel reception told this reporter in the lobby that Malcolm X was engaged, but Michael X was available if he wanted to talk to him.

The reporter spoke to me on the telephone and asked if he could have a word with me since Malcolm was occupied. He came up to my room, somewhat intrigued, and opened the conversation by asking if I was Malcolm's brother. I told him not really, that it was just a term by which we addressed each other. He asked my nationality and when I told him he said he hadn't realised there were any Black Muslims in Britain. I was rather amused by this misunderstanding and I told him I couldn't really say anything to him, that it was Malcolm he'd have to see. Shortly after that Malcolm rang to call me over to the press conference and we went together.

I listened to Malcolm dealing with the questions from the press with vigour and aplomb. The reporters would ask him if he hadn't at some time or place said something about black men taking up guns or some such violent remark, and did he still think this way. He would very patiently tell them that he did say something like that, but he had said it for such-and-such a reason in such-and-such a context, which put it in a completely different light. There were lots of questions and answers like that, but, unfortunately, nobody printed what he'd said in the papers next day. Instead they seized on a hypothetical comment he'd made about gas ovens in England and took it right out of context. I should have learned from that, ready for when I started to work with my own organisation. But I didn't at first. I suffered, too, from reporters taking phrases I had used and lifting them right out of context, which would make me sound like a terrifying character.

Birmingham was a new and interesting scene for me. After the press conference, I listened to Malcolm's speech on the problem of human—rather than civil—rights of the American Negro and heard the tumultuous applause which followed and then I ate with him and a number of the students in a Moslem restaurant. By the time we were in the train heading back to London, I was completely convinced that a branch of his Afro-American Unity organisation should be set up in London as it had been already in Paris. When it became apparent that he was leading up to ask me if I would work with an African he had in mind to set up an Organisation of Afro-Anglo Unity, I was ready to start working out strategy.

Malcolm was impressive not only because of his oratorical skill and fire, but because he made a lot of sense, too. His constant theme, now, was one of human rights for the black man and how any organisation to fight for these rights in the parts of the world where people were deprived of them must be set up on an international basis. Unity, he pointed out, was strength, and he warned of the white man's strategy of setting up black men as puppet leaders so that the black people were divided amongst themselves and never really achieved anything. He was very analytical and I never knew him to be caught out. The slightest point he made he could back to the hilt if necessary from the facts and figures in his little black bag.

The next day—the fourth of what had already become a close friendship—Malcolm and I spent several hours visiting the various black centres in London and putting our plan across to the West Indians we met. We found a whole lot of enthusiasm. Malcolm never tried to make a conversion the whole time I knew him. He told facts and let them do it for him. It was a technique which produced dividends. We were so successful in our initial attempt to drum up support that we began to work out organisational details and a time schedule which would culminate in Malcolm's return to London in the summer to attend the public launching of the organisation in Trafalgar Square.

During the day, I accompanied him to the mosque in Regent's Park when he went for prayer. It was the first time I had ever been inside a mosque and I was struck by the atmosphere of simple peace within. No statues, figurines or emblems to obtrude. Nothing but a carpet.

I asked Malcolm what I should do and he said : 'Sit down. It's your place.'

I did as he said, squatting down in the middle of the mosque while he prayed, and feeling more at peace than I had for a very long time. Before we left, I went to the mosque library and asked for some books on Islam. I wanted to know what it was all about.

That night, before Malcolm was due to leave the next day, we had a get-together at a friend's house and talked about a lot of things we hadn't touched on before. The Jews, for instance. Although he never came off his black-white thing, Malcolm had reached the stage where he was no longer making total generalisations about people. He had discovered in the Middle East that there were good people whose skins were white and he was also finding out that there were Jews and Jews. He had even developed a great amount of respect for some he'd met who were very different from the grasping Harlem shopkeepers by whom he'd judged the race in the past. He liked Nancy, as a case in point. 'She's a very nice girl,' he told me.

We also talked about the Negro middle class in the United States, and Negro writers. He felt that the conformism of the middle class Negro in America was an enormous loss to the race as a whole. 'It's a terrible waste,' he said. 'There's so much that these people of education and training could be doing to lift the black man up.' And he thought a lot of Negro writers were wasting their talent with endless intellectualising. 'They're going round and round in circles.'

One of the last things we spoke about was assassination. He told us about times in America when cars would be following him about, and he remembered one night in particular, slowing down his car outside his house and seeing people in the shadows of the doorway opposite. He kept going, parked the car elsewhere and climbed into his home over the back wall. On another occasion he was returning from a lecture in the country and the driver drew his attention to the fact that a car seemed to be following them. When they reached a lonely road, the car behind started to draw up on them and Malcolm said he knew 'this was it'. In desperate inspiration he stuck his cane through the side window as if it were a rifle—and the tailing car slowed down and dropped out of sight.

I would listen to his stories and wonder if it wasn't all melodrama, yet he spoke with such seriousness and conviction that it was very difficult not to believe him.

He mentioned that when he returned to the States he was going down south. Nancy told him to be careful and he replied that if anything happened to him it wouldn't happen in the south and he doubted if it would happen at the hands of a white racist.

'If a white man shot me in the south, it would make me a martyr,' he said, 'and they wouldn't want that. No. When it happens, it will happen in the north at the hands of a black man.'

Those were some of the last words Malcolm said to me. A few weeks later he was shot down—in the north, by a black man.

18

When Malcolm left, I set systematically to work. In addition to talking with West Indians at the various centres, I had a simple manifesto printed in which I stressed the theme of unity among black men in Britain and appealed for membership of the proposed organisation. I put it up in restaurants, barbers' shops, gaming houses, billiard halls—everywhere. I worked non-stop for two weeks and the result was fantastic. I was deluged with applications for membership. It was exhilarating to realise so many people cared.

I was sitting down to write a letter to Malcolm describing our success when a telephone call came through from America to tell me he'd been shot. I was stunned. I didn't really believe it. I had to turn on the radio to convince myself. I listened to the news and it was true—Malcolm was dead.

Very soon the phone started ringing and I was inundated with queries from newspapermen who remembered they'd met us together in Birmingham and wanted to know what I had to say about Malcolm's death. I was not terribly keen to talk about it, but I figured the best epitaph for Malcolm was to push things forward and I finally saw someone from the *Sunday Times*. The resultant article was all about 'Britain's Black Militants'. We were in business.

I was terribly shocked by Malcolm's death. I was hit hard by it. But death is a fact I've discovered I can live with. It's something that's going to happen. And that's it. Assassination is an occupational hazard of all leaders.

The only thing I could do was work harder. I got into a new pattern of leafletting an area, hiring a church hall and then talking to the audience about my plans. This brought me many offers of help from some excellent people. Three of them who really helped me get the organisation going were an Indian accountant from Guyana named Roy Sawh, the Guyanian writer, Jan Carew and an Indian graduate from Bombay University, Abdullah Patel.

Roy Sawh was an aggressive little man of thirty-four who looked ten years younger. He had his own following and had been preaching more or less the same line as mine at Hyde Park Corner. He had very strong feelings about the plight of the black man in this country and felt that the only way we would get things done was in unity. He turned up at one of my meetings and, after listening to me speak, came along to offer his services. I didn't know very much about him except that he'd had two years' training as an organiser in Russia and was disillusioned about that, although he didn't like to talk about it. Apart from that I knew he worked all day and drank and danced all night. He was an extremely good-looking man, a neat dresser and very fond of the ladies. When he started to work for me full-time I discovered two more things—that he was a great crowd-puller and that his energy was fantastic.

Jan Carew was very different. He was reserved—even shy—and, although he, too, was a very good speaker, his particular quality was a clear, analytical mind. Jan also had quite a following of young people—mostly students—and when he came over to help, naturally he brought them with him. He was a very attractive person, to youth in particular : a good-looking thirty-seven, six feet two inches tall and very strong. Physical fitness was an important thing to him. He was a black belt in judo and was constantly encouraging young people to look after their bodies and to praetise judo and karate. He felt a young organisation, such as ours, must have an efficient physical wing.

Abdullah Patel was different from both the others. He looked like any little Indian factory worker or bus driver, and, although he was an honours graduate, he was working in a factory here, which was the only kind of work he could get. He was a devout Moslem and a very hard worker; the kind of man who is only happy if he's on the go up to twenty hours a day. He travelled from town to town for the organisation—speaking very persuasively in Urdu and Gujerati—and existing on only shillings a day, which was a valuable ability in the early days when we had little money to work with.

We began to have regular meetings to discuss details of organisation and policy, making mistakes and learning from them as we went along. We concentrated on the London area, collecting names and seeing people, drafting literature, considering ways of raising funds. We expanded rapidly and found so many problems that we had to open an office in Islington and form a full-time executive with myself as president and Patel as vice president.

One of our principal early problems was finding a suitable name for the organisation. We decided we wanted something different from the usual collection of initials and were searching for a sound that would appeal to the black man. This proved to be difficult. Mau Mau—purely as a sound—is a case in point, of an organisation whose name would be attractive to black people. But we needed something which would apply in Britain.

We eventually came up with Racial Adjustment Action Society, whose initials form the word RAAS. This abbreviation has great appeal as a sound and it also has various interesting connotations.

In the first place RAAS is a West Indian word for a menstrual blood cloth. It has some symbolic significance in view of the way the black man has been drained of his life blood for so long. In the second place there is the similar African word *ras* (from the Arabic *ra's*—head) meaning Ruler or Leader. The Committee thought it very suitable.

We had hardly sorted ourselves out when something happened to turn the national spotlight on the organisation and boost it throughout the country.

The Courtauld's textile factory in Preston suddenly had problems. The firm's nine hundred coloured workers went on strike en bloc after a row with the management. And the driving force behind the action was Abdullah Patel, who worked there.

The strike was caused by a sudden and arbitrary decision of the management that their workers should operate one-and-a-half machines apiece instead of one—giving them fifty per cent more work for very little extra pay. The move was against all trade union practice and the workers objected. Patel organised the strike and called on RAAS for help. Frankly, none of us on the executive had any idea how to deal with industrial action of this kind. We might easily have wasted a lot of time running in wrong directions if help hadn't come from an unexpected quarter.

In the midst of our discussions at my flat in Primrose Hill, the telephone rang and it was Oscar Brown junior. I had met Oscar in the Maria-Angela days and we had a nice friendship going on. He was a rare phenomenon—a Negro with blue eyes. And he had a sparkling personality. I dug him and I dug his voice and records, and I was very happy that he phoned me whenever he was passing through London. On this occasion he had just flown into town from Chicago to star at the Cool Elephant. I told him to come right on over.

He arrived in the middle of our talks on the strike and sat listening while Nancy made him something to eat. We were rambling around the subject in some confusion, displaying just how green we were, getting absolutely nowhere. Oscar contained himself politely for a while and then the spirit moved behind those blue eyes and he said: 'Michael, gentlemen, do you mind if I make a few suggestions?'

We were ready to accept any suggestions from anyone and we gave him our full attention while, to my utter astonishment, he told us exactly what we had to do. His advice covered everything from the type of specialist lawyer required to the details of setting up a factory workers' committee. Up to that point I had looked upon Oscar as a great artist and entertainer and our conversation had been confined to music and the pleasures of life. I had never connected him with civil rights, politics, racial questions—and now he revealed himself as something of an expert in these fields.

When I probed into this unknown part of him, I discovered that Oscar had had a great deal of experience with organisations in Chicago and was bang up to date on everything that was happening on the racial scene in the States. He taught me a lot about the situation there, urging me not to confine myself simply to Malcolm's view of things, but to look at the other organisations and what they were doing: Martin Luther King, CORE, SNCC and the rest. He gave me lots of names and addresses to write to, including the editor of *Mr Muhammed Speaks*, the Black Muslim newspaper. Some time later I discovered that his father, Oscar Brown senior, was Elijah Muhammed's lawyer.

Before he left, Oscar showed yet another aspect of his talent. For some time we had been printing leaflets advertising our meetings and aims. They were not terribly well done and, as we did separate ones for each town we visited, production was proving a costly business. We needed a standard leaflet. While we continued to discuss the Preston strike that night, Oscar cast his eyes over our literature, borrowed a pencil and turned out a leaflet that was precisely what we wanted : attractive and well-designed, presenting all the information we wanted to get across in simple, concise terms. We adopted it immediately as the form we'd been seeking. Some months later, Oscar Brown junior, as anonymous artist, appeared on the cover of *Spectator* (November 12th, 1965) when the magazine copied the leaflet as illustration to an article on RAAS.

So, thanks to Oscar, we got working on the Preston strike without any hang-ups. I went up to help Patel work out the financial structure and engage the necessary lawyers, while Jan Carew and Roy Sawh looked after things in London.

Press interest was fantastic. Everybody was writing about the strike because there had never been anything like it before in the country. Television was also keen on coverage and one company chartered a couple of aeroplanes to take its crew from London. Jan and Roy were also planning a visit at that moment and the company invited them along. The strikers were told Jan and Roy were on their way up in a private plane and when they saw them step out followed by a television crew, seven hundred of them joined RAAS on the spot.

From then on the press started to talk about a racialist strike and tie it up with me as if I'd brought it about. I'd done no such thing. Industrial war was the last activity we would have chosen for an organisation which was still trying to get off the ground.

With this talk about race, the strikers suddenly had a visit from one of the West Indian High Commissioners in London. He appeared at the local theatre we had hired for the evening meetings of the strikers' action group and was given leave to address the strikers. Without having consulted management or workers he began forcefully to persuade them to go back to work. The basis of his case was that this was England and they had to do things the English way. 'I will talk to the management,' he said.

When some of the younger elements began to argue with him, he left. But he had been very persuasive. It was the first time many of the West Indians up there had ever seen any of their

High Commissioners. However, of a total of ninety West Indians, about seventy went back—a very small proportion of the whole strike.

The High Commissioner didn't talk to the management. He just went back to London. I was horrified by his behaviour. I can't think why he felt he had to get involved. Even in London, for every one West Indian the High Commissioners have helped there are thousands for whom they have done nothing. Most of the West Indian High Commissioners in this country have completely neglected the West Indian worker. Many are too busy going to the Queen's garden parties to do anything for the man in the street.

West Indians in Britain are probably among the most abandoned people in the world. Abandoned by the host country and abandoned by their own countries, too. This is a shame because in the case of some of the islands their nationals here send more money home than the total internal earnings of the island; the home economy would collapse without them. But the High Commissioners don't know them and don't appear to want to know them. I never heard of the High Commissioners concerning themselves with the problems of their nationals in, say, Brixton or Notting Hill, or anywhere else. It may seem a hard statement to make, but you could pick out any dozen West Indian workers on any street corner in any part of Britain and see what they say about it. The High Commissioners are out of touch.

Well, the High Commissioner notwithstanding, RAAS organised the strikers into a disciplined body. We held meetings to raise money for strike pay and our spiralling expenses, briefed lawyers and arranged discussions between the workers' committee and the management. We worked very hard and kept morale high so that a united front could be maintained. The result was that after a few weeks a solution was found which was acceptable to both sides and the workers went back to their jobs with a measure of satisfaction.

With all this publicity, RAAS appeared to be a terribly powerful organisation and we were much in demand. Groups from all over the country were contacting us, asking for help with their various problems and we began to receive up to four hundred letters of application for membership every week.

Throughout the strike, the press had refused to call me Michael de Freitas. They preferred to perpetuate the fiction of Michael X

—a Black Muslim label whose militant ring was no doubt considered to have greater appeal to their readers. Even when I was converted to Islam soon after the strike, and chose the name Michael Abdul Malik, Michael X lived on as a public image.

I didn't really choose the new name myself. It was selected by the Preston factory workers. Malik is the Arabic for God or king, and Abdul means servant. The strikers had observed me working long hours in Preston and they said : 'This man works all the time; truly he is the servant of God.'

The mechanics of conversion to Islam are very simple : you read the first part of the Koran, which says in essence that there is no God but Allah and Mohammed is his prophet; you recognise Mohammed as the last prophet of God; you recognise Islam —which in Arabic means 'entering into peace'—as the true religion. You declare your conviction in the presence of other Moslems—and that's it. My own conversion had been building up since I met Malcolm. I had been reading about Islam, corresponding about it with the Nation of Islam and attending the mosque in Regent's Park. I'd found a number of very beautiful things in it : the Koran itself; the life of Abu Bakr, one of the successors of Mohammed, who was a Negro and said : 'If a Negro slave is appointed to rule over you, hear him and obey him, though his head should be like that of a dried raisin.' I was also impressed by the discipline—of which I'd had very little in my own life—and the example of Malcolm's own transformation after becoming a Moslem. But above all I found it so much more compatible with my own nature than the Christian faith I'd grown up with. It got across to me.

There had always been some kind of intangible God creature in my mind. I had never denied this. But the Christian God was just unacceptable as he was presented to me. From the beginning I was very angry with the Catholic Church in the West Indies. I was sick of seeing my mother doling out large sums of money to the priests to pay for my sins when I needed that money— and she did too—so much more than they. Those priests had so much and yet they took so readily from people who had so little. And they lied, those priests. They preached brotherly love while they practised racialism. They preached purity while they practised licentiousness. As an acolyte I was able to observe their behaviour away from the altar : the mauling and kissing of the ladies, which was very far from fatherly. And those chicks weren't going to their bedrooms for confession, man. Whatever they said, those Christian priests from Italy and Ireland, they acted the very opposite. And I just couldn't accept that those vicious men were going to heaven any more than I could accept that I was heading for hell and damnation.

There were so many things about Christianity I couldn't get along with. This Christian business about the promised land, for example. I didn't want anything after I died; I wanted it now. That's how Christians have kept black people deprived for centuries—talking about the promised land and rewards in heaven. Nor was I prepared to turn the other cheek. I don't believe in it and I never did.

In Islam I found things were very different. Islam stands for getting things done—now. And for doing them yourself. It's a religion of today : do this and your present life will be better. I don't like the idea of leaving things for God to do. You have to do things yourself if you really want them done.

Christ as presented by the Christians never rang true with me either. I can't take Christ as the son of God any more than anyone else is exclusively the son of God. We're all sons of God. In the Koran there's another Christ who's just one of the prophets. I dig that cat in the Koran just as I dig Mohammed, who was an organiser extraordinary.

Islam is a religion that makes sense to me. It says that God is within you—and that's a God I can deal with. I don't see him in Islam as an omnipotent being sitting up on a cloud and throwing thunderbolts at people who don't toe the line. Nor do I see him as the Christian God who threatens me with fire and hell for not going to church on Sunday when it may be cold and I don't have shoes. Nobody threatens you in Islam. You live the day as clean as you can. God is within and it's a question of how to bring Him out in order to get better results.

The discipline was good for me, too. There are certain things in Islam which you can't do, like drinking alcohol. I used to drink a fair amount and it really did need discipline to stop. I used to love pork, as well. In fact spare ribs was my favourite dish. But that's another thing I haven't touched since. Discipline in these things can lead on to discipline in others.

And there was one immediately practical reason why Islam was so good for me. Before Malcolm's death, when my organisation first started, I had him to call on about the countless problems which kept arising. When he died there was nobody I could turn to and yet more and more people were coming to me with problems to which I had no answer. But the Koran did.

Malcolm had often talked about the 'wonderful book' in which there was the answer to any problem. I would read the Koran and search for these answers. And there I would find them.

19

The strike had given us star quality. When we returned to London at its successful conclusion we had to increase the size of our central committee to deal with our mushrooming growth. Roy gave up his platform in Hyde Park to become our full-time National Organiser and Patel left his job at the factory to go on the road with other field workers in one of the several teams we sent out to tour all major towns with coloured populations.

At the same time, speakers from RAAS were in enormous demand : by universities, political parties, Zionists, Moslems. The whole world seemed to want to know what we were doing. I was even invited to a Cambridge Union debate to speak for the motion 'that the Americans should get out of Vietnam'. I lost the motion by some ten votes, but it was quite an experience.

Patel and Roy between them did a fantastic job on the provincial tours and membership was increasing like mad. Our policy was not to charge—that every black man in the country had a right to be a member. This resulted in us having 65,000 members on paper after a year's work. And our problems increased in proportion.

All our members wanted things done for them, from advice on divorce to help with housing difficulties. We had a constant stream of invitations to speak at little towns throughout the country and our publicity was prodigious. We had too much of it, too sensational. After the press had splashed a threat to blow up the hall in which I was due to speak in Nottingham, I kept quiet about the countless threats to kill me which flowed into the office. We just kept a curiosity file of them. The fact was that we needed a rest from publicity so that we could take quiet stock and decide what we were actually organising for, create something constructive. Raising funds had also become a major preoccupation. Our mail was staggering, with inland postage stamps alone costing us between £30 and £40 a week and helpers typing around the clock.

When we put out a call for voluntary help, we found that a lot of young white girls would turn up to help with the typing, but there was precious little response from black people. It emerged that whereas white people were often quite happy to do voluntary work, the black man was only prepared to work for wages —which is not too hard to figure.

We were in something of a dilemma about the amount of work and how much it was costing. We kept appealing for funds, but the money we got was nowhere near enough to keep us going. The problem was overcome temporarily by a chance meeting.

While Oscar was still in London, I went with him one night to spend a social evening with friends of his in Mayfair. Among the gathering were a number of wealthy white ladies and I started chatting with one of them, who seemed very interested in what I was doing. I shall call her Carmen—a beautiful woman with a lovely, supple body. She was a widow and now, at the age of thirty, had all the time in the world to indulge herself. She had just returned from abroad when I met her and had a marvellous tan. I found her poised and witty and a good listener. She professed a great interest in racial problems and what could be done to offset them in this country. We met again to discuss this. We talked about the possibility of staging a show at the Albert Hall with her money and my promotion. I reckoned we could get Oscar and Dick Gregory to take part and then share the proceeds in some agreed proportion. We went on meeting about this, although it never came to anything, and then she asked if she could do anything to help the organisation. I asked her how she meant and she said she meant financially. I told her we were certainly having difficulty and that if she felt like helping us out we'd be very grateful. At that, she opened her handbag and gave me a bundle of £10 notes.

I went off to Nottingham to speak after that and when I returned to London a couple of days later she told me she had been talking to a number of her Mayfair friends and that if I wanted to approach them for money I should be able to get quite a lot of backing from them. I had misgivings about this and I explained how determined we had always been to confine the organisation and its workings to black people. I went into the reasons for this in some detail. Carmen listened attentively and then shook her head. She doubted very much, she said, whether the people she had in mind would hand over large sums of money without having some say in the running of the organisation. As if to separate herself and her motives from these people, she then wrote me out a cheque for £500, which I gratefully accepted.

I presented the cheque and the £10 notes to the committee that same night. I have no doubt the ponce element produced in the black man by the ghetto was with me that night. I told them the money was from 'a woman who likes me'. I could have simply said it was money from a benefactor, but somehow I couldn't resist adding the sexual bit. I think my mind went back to Clarence and his conquests and I had the feeling how clever I was. I saw their affinity with me shining in the eyes of the committee as they accepted the gifts and one of them even said: 'That's a good thing.'

At this point I outlined the dilemma we were in due to money and work problems and astonished everybody by suggesting there was a simple answer—that we make greater use of sympathetic white people. I put up the idea of associate membership so that we could harness the help, in terms of both finance and voluntary work, we were likely to get from the whites.

Not a soul agreed with me. They wouldn't hear of it.

This was hardly surprising as my teachings all along had been on the theme of non-white participation. I popped out the contrary view without building up to it and the committee members fell over themselves to offer more personal help rather than dilute the colour of the organisation.

A few evenings later I was speaking in Manchester on the theme of the West Indian woman and her matriarchal role in West Indian society—I was getting away from the sole theme of unity—when, running my glance along the front rows of the audience, I was startled to see Carmen's face. After the meeting she waited and asked if she could drive me to Liverpool where I was due to speak next day. Usually I travelled by train, but I saw no point in turning down this offer of a comfortable lift and we set off. As we were passing through a village half way between the two cities, Carmen slowed the car and said: 'I know a nice little hotel here. Why don't we spend the night here, together?'

This was hardly unexpected. When we first met, I was so involved with organisation troubles that I wasn't really thinking of indulging in any sexual adventure with her and I blinded myself to what I was letting myself in for. But she was very pretty and the fact that she was giving me money did increase her attractiveness as far as I was concerned. As the relationship developed, it had become obvious we wanted to go to bed with each other. So we went to bed. And it was swinging.

But when the affair went on for a few weeks while I was popping in and out of London on lecture tours, the terms of reference changed completely. From being a chick it was nice to make, Carmen became for me purely a source of income. The sums of money she gave me got larger and larger in a scene that came close to reminding me of my old poncing days. It was only then that I saw the real effect the ghetto had achieved in reducing my humanity and enabling me to look on a woman as a commodity. The pressures in the ghetto are so hard that they dehumanise people. And they do it in such a way that someone has to keep working at helping them become human again. That's probably why Malcolm worked so much in the ghettoes he knew so well.

I took another long look at myself and the sight wasn't a very pleasant one. The sordidness of the whole affair made it impossible for me to talk to the committee any more about where the money came from. I simply handed it over and everybody was pleased that the bills were being paid and didn't ask any questions. With every cheque received, my peace of mind disintegrated a little more. As I moved about the country, finding life more and more unbearable, so my speeches became more and more bitter. They reached a new peak of being anti-white. I was terribly hard on poncing and the selling of bodies; I had a lot to say about the awful traps black men fell into, which were terribly degrading for them. I was quite nasty about the women involved. It was myself I was flaying.

I didn't feel a lot of guilt towards Nancy. Men the world over will go for an extra-marital relationship and I was on the road, moving, and there was this attractive woman turning up unexpectedly. Carmen fully understood that I had a nice woman I lived with and she was happy for any little joy she could find within that context. I could salve my conscience by sending Nancy a dozen roses. I was really so involved with work, anyway, that I had no time to consider that aspect of the affair. I didn't intend to return to London and conduct some sort of double life. Carmen and I were just something that was happening in the country. But the 'necessary exploitation', as I termed it in my own mind, was becoming something I couldn't live with. Something had to give—even if it meant losing the big income I'd been getting for the organisation.

So, finally, I had a long, serious talk with Carmen, pointing out that there was no future in the way we were going and saying that we should end the relationship. There were no half measures about her reaction. She promptly had a nervous breakdown and was confined in a London clinic. Far from not seeing her again, I found myself in the unexpected role of daily visitor bearing flowers.

However, when she came out she took off for her beloved Mediterranean and was much happier. We are good friends now.

With the departure of Carmen, RAAS had no more income and I called an executive meeting and pointed out how much the organisation was costing. I said we were likely to suffer from now on, that I required more help from them and that we should make provision for members to pay. The debate on this continued for three hours before it was decided that membership should cost ten shillings a year for those who could afford it. We sent out a questionnaire on this and more than seventy per cent of the members objected.

We had already discovered that many black men were quite happy to sit back and think they'd pulled their weight simply by announcing themselves as members. This really meant very little. What we began asking ourselves was how many active members we had.

After a long hard thinking session, we decided to concentrate on having wholly active members and to regard non-active members as dead weight. We set about weeding out the hard core people and whittled our following down to just over 2,000—which was a manageable number for our resources and meant we could really get things done. We began by drafting out fresh policy points. And in place of the one-page leaflets we'd brought out to date, we began producing complete booklets for people

F

to study, giving information about everything we were doing and planned to do.

Among our aims, apart from uniting coloured people in Britain and guaranteeing their human rights, were the promotion of trades, industries and business run by black people to make them less dependent on white capital; the establishment of centres for physical, educational, social and cultural activities; creation of co-operative housing projects; encouragement for black people to participate in their professional associations and trade unions; provision of legal advice, either free or on low terms, and professional advice for the management of businesses; incorporation of a building society to make mortgage advances to black people at reasonable rates of interest. These were some of the most specifically practical points in a long programme which was intended to help give the black man a fair deal.

In writing up the constitution of RAAS, I also finally succeeded in including associate membership for whites.

I had been studying the various race organisations in the United States, and smaller ones in Britain, and I found they almost all had white membership. I watched the way they operated and I attended a major meeting of the largest of them in this country. The leader of this organisation was black, but it was completely staffed with white people, including a number of white lawyers. I have no doubt it is a more efficient body than RAAS, but I don't suppose black men have learned a thing from it.

This particular meeting was supposed to present it as a showpiece to the nation and since there were so few black members, the leaders had had a scramble to get black men on the platform. One of the people they'd raked in was an actor and film star. In the midst of the general back-slapping and morale-boosting, he made a short speech as his contribution to race relations.

'I'll tell you the way to get harmonious race relations in this country,' he said. 'You must encourage the Queen to adopt a black baby. We must petition her to do this.'

An embarrassed hush fell on the gathering and everyone stared at him so that he began repeating his suggestion with his voice rising. . . . 'There's no other way out of this. We must petition her!' My enthusiasm got the better of me at this ridiculous idea and I called out: 'Don't encourage her to adopt one. Let her have one!'—a satirical comment that seemed to get everyone very angry.

The black leader of this predominantly white organisation once got very vicious about me on the BBC and described me as a drug pedlar and gangster'. I retaliated in an interview by describing him as a 'very charming gentleman' and his organisation as a 'very gentlemanly association'.

All this is by way of saying that I can see there should be some way in which a black organisation could benefit from the experience and help of white friends, but I don't see any organisation so far, either here or in America, which has the answer to how it should be done. The associate member clause for RAAS was my attempt to bridge the gap and I was spurred on to insert it because of the help Colin MacInnes, the writer, was giving me. I had met him when he interviewed me for *Encounter* and we kept bumping into each other all over the place since he was very much involved with the coloured scene. I would find him in West Indian flats here and there, sitting on the floor in his sweater, jeans and tennis shoes, his pale, lined face intense as he argued point after point. He was a terribly hard worker and would turn out night and day at any hour to visit people, to go bail for those who were arrested and to advise in all manner of things with no kind of recognition for his services. He has so much energy, wants to do so much and so hates to see people making mistakes that he might be one of the most dangerous of white liberals if it weren't for his understanding of the black man. Colin really is interested in black *people*. One of the ways he shows this is in trying to learn the language of the black man. He seeks out the meaning of West Indian words. Where most people would be lost listening to some West Indian conversations, Colin wouldn't, and if you speak a man's language you're sure to understand him better. As it is, Colin comes as near to being colourless as anyone I know. Of course, there's no such thing as a completely colourless person, although the white liberal and the black bourgeois talk a lot of bullshit about it. At best, black and white can have enough things in common and enough joy to share between them to be colourless most of the time. But complete disregard of colour can't be attained with the world in its present situation. It's impossible to forget who you are all the time, the pigeon hole you've been placed in, the imposed divisions people have created in which colour is such a prominent example.

No white man can know how a black man feels when he walks down a street, and when white men ask me what I would do if

I were in their position I can't possibly say, because I'm not. In race riots I have been walking down a street and seen not individuals coming towards me, but featureless whites. White people have told me exactly the same thing in reverse. This is the most frightening situation of all and one we should do everything we can to avoid.

Associate membership of RAAS, with Colin MacInnes as an example, may be one way of doing this. An associate member can only advise; he has no voting power. The black man has to make the decisions and do the work. So far Colin is our only associate member. We wish there were more—and no doubt there will be.

In the course of development, it has emerged that the best way to ensure that the black man from the ghetto will work in an organisation is to make him an officer. Give a man a title and he will be very active, determined to live up to it. So we began to create a number of independent but associated groups, the most important of which is solely for handling the legal defence of people who are arrested. It is called 'Defence' and it operates in Notting Hill with Colin MacInnes as public relations officer.

The necessity for Defence may be illustrated by the true story of a Jamaican who lived in the ghetto. He was a carpenter and had been working on a job during the afternoon. Before going home he spent a few hours chatting with people in cafés and gaming houses and it was night by the time he set out for his house. At a street corner he was stopped by two policemen who examined his bag of tools and asked him where he was going with them. The Jamaican became so frightened that he had no idea what to say. He simply wanted to run from this threatening authority, and he began to look very like the 'suspicious character' the police no doubt thought he was. He was taken to the police station and charged with having housebreaking instruments in his possession with intent to break into premises of some kind. This terrified him even more, and when he was put in a cell he was literally speechless from fear.

Appearing before the magistrate next morning, he was still practically inarticulate, was told not to mumble and could hardly utter even his name. He was sentenced to three months imprisonment.

No man should have this absolute fear in relation to authority and Defence was formed to operate throughout the twenty-four hours with a panel of lawyers on tap, together with responsible black men ready to help anyone who was arrested and go bail for him if necessary. The arrested man had only to ring a number which had been posted on boards in cafés and gaming houses throughout the ghetto. The group is not interested in whether a man is guilty or innocent, but simply in ensuring that he gets legal representation to avoid miscarriages of justice.

Since Defence was formed, we have had a rather similar case to that of the Jamaican carpenter. On this occasion three black men were driving into London from the country and ran out of petrol. They hadn't enough money on them to buy any more so they parked at the roadside and decided to sleep there until morning. A police car found them and the patrol began to question them. The men got frightened and gave confused answers. When the police opened the boot of the car, they found a crowbar, a screwdriver and other tools which the men, who were building workers, used in their jobs. They were charged with the same offence as the Jamaican.

The difference in this case was that one of the three knew about Defence and telephoned the number. We were able to get a lawyer to the station almost immediately, together with a West Indian interpreter. Once the men saw a black face they felt safer and began to talk and explain their true circumstances. They were acquitted in court next day.

20

Quite apart from my conviction that white people should not play any major part in black organisations, I have always been ready to co-operate with them in any worthwhile venture outside that context.

Two such projects with which I have been and still am involved are the experimental London Free School and Alexander Trocchi's 'sigma'.

I got tied up with sigma in my early days with Nancy. She asked me to get home early one evening as this friend of hers, a writer whom she admired, was coming to see her and she wanted me to meet him.

I duly turned up and there was Alex Trocchi sitting in this great black overcoat down to his knees painting a small piece of driftwood in bright, plastic paints. I had already read and liked his first novel, *Young Adam*, and I looked with interest at another man who had lived most of his life outside society in one way or another. A junkie of some years' standing, he was rather skinny as they tend to be, but there was a lot of strength in his striking, bony face and sometimes those deepset eyes under their bushy brows could be almost hypnotic.

We shook hands and after a few introductory exchanges he began talking in his slow, deliberate Scots voice about his travels —he had recently returned from the United States—about Spain, where he was going to meet his wife and child, about his editorship of the expatriate magazine, *Merlin*, in the Paris of the 'fifties, about art and life and about the project sigma.

The significance and ramifications of sigma did not seem clear cut to me, but Alex was very emphatic in his statements and appeared to have no doubts at all about the workability of the idea which he saw as a global cultural revolt which would 'seize the grids of expression and the power-house of the mind' to create a more conscious and creative world and have done with 'self-deceit and public hypocrisies'. Writers, for example, would have their work published by sigma with a percentage of profits going back into the project, whose manifestations would include 'action universities' run by members with branches throughout the world. Alex, who had been discovering much of the best contemporary writing for years, was quite sure the organisation would soon have a complete monopoly of literature, cutting out middlemen in the process. Belonging to the organisation would inspire members to work and play together rather than against one another—in contrast to the cut-throat world outside. I think Alex hoped a new-type man would emerge—and he could be right. One early idea was to rent a big house in the country for some ten families and perhaps have a shop window in London for the display of work. But, as with most such schemes, the big problem at the time was money.

I found Alex interesting and very likeable and said I would like to help him find some premises. He said yes, as if he'd heard that story before and I had to explain that I was quite sincere in wanting to help him and that I probably could. He said there was the problem that he might not have any money since his income from writing was rather irregular and I said not to worry, we could always work that out.

All the time we were talking he'd been painting this piece of driftwood, filling in one colour over another, constantly developing the pattern. Before he left I asked him when it would be finished and his smiling answer was typical of the man : 'Never. Nothing is ever finished. There's always something else you can do.'

Two weeks later I was at a friend's place when Nancy rang and said Alex was back in town and wanted to take me up on my offer of premises. I was taken by surprise so I went to see my wife in Islington and asked her if she would give one of the rooms in the house to Alex and his family until I could make other arrangements. Desirée was quite happy about it, saying she would enjoy the company, so Alex moved in, insisting that he must pay something. We finally worked out a nominal rent which was satisfactory to both of us.

I began to see a whole lot of Alex. He was terribly articulate and I liked a whole lot of things he said and did, particularly a project of his called the International Collection which arose out of the sigma idea. This was to be a very unconventional type of collection of manuscripts, paintings, sculptures etcetera by sympathetic writers and artists, given freely by them, which would constitute an international force.

Alex was the only serious drug addict I had met at that time. I had known a lot of people in a sad state in the East End, but nobody who claimed that it was a good thing to do and who functioned well and worked hard the way Alex did. He used a great quantity of heroin and cocaine, taking a fix every half hour wherever he could find room in his scarred veins to inject. All the time he was writing and translating and meeting people and talking. I was very interested. It was his scene and I respected it.

Alex went on living at the house in Islington and the place I'd hoped to get for him never materialised. He was unable to do anything about it himself due to lack of money. Money was constantly on the point of arriving for him and then it seldom did until the projects in hand had lost their initial vitality. A writer's lot can be a very hard one.

There were lots of minor projects Alex was always talking about, but his own situation was often a mess financially and this tended to stymie their evolution.

One time when I had quite a bit of money, I asked Alex if he'd accept some from me and how much he needed. He said £100 would put him straight. I told him I would give him lots of £50 and with some reluctance he accepted my offer. He wanted the £100 at one time, but I had the feeling I should give it him in two stages, so I gave him the first £50 and he was desperate or gracious enough to be very pleased.

About a week later I hadn't turned up with the other half and I received a beautiful letter from Alex asking why the hell I was keeping his money from him. I went to see him and asked what he'd done with the first sum—which was rather stupid as I'd given it him with no strings attached and he had no reason to account to me. He got quite indignant. 'What have I done with it!' he roared. 'What have I done with it. . . ! I've bought flowers for a beautiful woman—that's what I've done with it!'

I'm glad to say he didn't hold the question against me.

Alex was most encouraging about my own writing, discussing essays I produced and constantly urging me to write more. One day I wrote a little ditty to him and he showed it to his wife, Lyn, saying: 'Look at this beautiful poem Michael's written for me.' From then on I was writing poetry and I took his advice and just wrote about the things I knew: my children, my wife, my own life. I tried to follow his other point of advice, too: not to be afraid of the truth.

I'm still one of the 'directors' of the International Collection and project sigma, together with William Burroughs, Felix Topolski, Robert Creeley and Ronald Laing, the psychiatrist. The idea still has to be made concrete. It may sound Utopian, but I think it could be a great thing given one good man to look after the business side.

My connection with the London Free School came some time later through one of the countless telephone calls I had from people trying to involve me in social projects—like wanting me to join a march to South Africa in protest against apartheid. This particular call was from a young man named John Hopkins who invited me to his flat in Queensway to discuss a new form of education which he hoped to put into operation in the area of Paddington and North Kensington. He mentioned a number of my friends who were interested in this experiment and would be at the meeting and I suppose that's the main reason I agreed to attend.

John Hopkins was a thin, intense twenty-one-year-old ex-public schoolboy who'd left Cambridge University because he was disillusioned with the form of education. Nervous energy radiated from him and I thought at the time that if this man put his mind to something he'd probably get it done. His flat was full of people like social workers, doctors, psychiatrists, teachers, all of whom were interested in the new idea which was being talked about. The educational side of the project was basically simple: to hold free classes on as many subjects as there were available teachers and to establish a sort of dialogue—a pooling of experience and knowledge—between teachers and pupils so that both would benefit. Beyond this, of course, were ramifications spreading from the fact of getting people in an area together to discuss their lives and their problems. The London Free School is, in fact, a social experiment.

Everybody at the meeting was terribly sincere and eager and I was caught up in the wave of enthusiasm. I talked a bit about the area and its needs as I saw them and I said I thought the idea a very interesting and workable one. John Hopkins—or, Hoppy, as he was generally called—asked me if I would take a class and I agreed to take one in basic English. I chose this subject because I knew the area was swarming with illiterates who didn't like the idea of people teaching them anything and I felt that if this two-way system got going they would find it acceptable.

We publicised our scheme at a large meeting in a local hall which was attended by well over a hundred people of all colours, and from there we began to set up lots of different classes.

I had my former gaming house basement lying empty with the rent paid and I gave it over to the Free School for an eighteen-month period; a local priest gave his church hall for use almost every day at a nominal rent; and a local woman contributed the lower part of her house. With this sort of provision, we were able to run a different class nearly every day in subjects like English, painting, mental health, debating, child welfare, economics, boxing . . . all manner of things.

My own classes had a degree of success which typified that of the whole school. My first class brought in a lot of middle-aged and elderly Irish people, a number of Africans and a solitary West Indian. They didn't even know the letters of the alphabet and they sat looking at me expectantly, wondering how the miracle was to be worked. I started off telling them about the value of education and how it could be related to their everyday lives and help their children, and then I went on to chat about my own experiences in the area, my life at sea and things like that. They seemed very interested in what I was saying and when I stopped and began asking them what they'd been doing with their lives, most of them were quite eager to talk about themselves. They told me all about the days of their youth in Ireland or Africa; how they remembered the days in Notting Hill when beer was a few pennies a pint and you could get a ha'pennyworth of chips at the fish and chip shops; how they'd dug gas main trenches for a living, or carried house bricks, or been a night watchman; how all their children had worked newspaper rounds to supplement the family income. I learned more social history, more vividly, than I'd have got out of any book and, in turn, I'd write on a blackboard the main points of what they were telling me and have them copy down the words. They did this laboriously at first, but with greater and greater fluency as they mastered the letters and words. And they did it with a degree of fascination which made learning easier for them than they'd ever imagined it could be. They were writing about their own lives. The words meant something for them in terms of their own experience and their interest was riveted in a way that no abstract presentation of English could have achieved.

Sometimes I would talk about some famous person who'd started life doing exactly the same sort of thing as my pupils. They would be able to have direct relations with that person and readily accept the increased vocabulary his life provided. The secret was always to relate the learning to something they could identify with.

From these discussions, many of their problems would be laid bare and they could be turned onto another class which could help—mental health or child welfare, for example. This led to our most successful and popular class which we called the Neighbourhood Service. During classes we found a lot of people talked about their housing problems and other difficulties relating to the area. Often these could not be approached in isolation; they would involve other things like education or how to budget, which only a comprehensive class on daily living could provide.

The Free School was so successful that it began to put out a regular paper of news and views called *The Grove*, whose circulation rose to 2,000. The visit of Mohammed Ali, the heavyweight boxing champion, also helped to focus interest on the School's activities and enabled us to raise money for other amenities like the provision of an adventure playground for children of the area—the only playground they have—on a piece of ground that's due to have a fly-over built on it some time in the future.

It was with this that we got the first inkling of official hostility. The local council, who had agreed to our request that the ground be used for the benefit of the children, said they would clear it of dangerous debris like the rusty old car bodies and lumps of jagged scrap iron with which it was littered. Suddenly, however, they seemed to show no further interest in the scheme and we got on with the job of clearing the site ourselves.

A little later, officers of Scotland Yard's Special Branch appeared in the area and visited a number of my colleagues in the Free School to advise them that I was a criminal, a subversive element and a generally dangerous character and that they should have nothing to do with me. This was, to say the least, upsetting for everyone and they called a meeting to discuss it. The outcome was a categorical decision that the Free School would not be pressurised by Scotland Yard or anyone else to get rid of one of their workers. Hoppy actually went to Scotland Yard to complain about their approach and got a verbal apology.

I can see there would be quite a few people in the area and outside who would object to me. There *was* my criminal past. There was the fact that I'd upset landlords in Notting Hill and some of them had long memories. And there was RAAS and my publicised uncompromising stand on black-white relations, which was something the press had built up rather than my own attitude.

Things came to a head when we decided to revive the Notting Hill Fair and Pageant—once a regular event—which had not taken place for more than a hundred years. The local council had promised a considerable grant towards this rebirth, but they stated they would only give this money if the Free School got rid of me as a subversive element. The School had been really depending on the money and I felt they would have to yield under this sort of pressure. But they refused point blank. I was very happy about this and it made me work that much harder.

The Fair happened eventually without the council's help. About 1,000 West Indians and 1,500 white people turned out in a real carnival atmosphere with floats, a steel band, poetry readings, jazz—all sorts of activities in which whites and blacks could have fun together. There were far more policemen around than one would have expected, but they were very polite. One inspector even came up to me and said : 'You are responsible for this? It's very nice.' But there was one bizarre note : a fire engine crowded with firemen, with hoses at the ready, slowly followed the West Indian steel band wherever it went. It was hard to understand its purpose. Some people thought it was part of the celebrations. Anyway it didn't upset anybody and the Fair went on for a week —a complete sell-out.

The work of the Free School is still going on and expanding— there are branches abroad now in places as far apart as Holland and the United States, and other interesting experiments have sprung from it, including publication of the iconoclastic newspaper, the *International Times*.

Others may describe us as Communists, Moslems, Provos or
any other label they like to think of. But our group has continued
to work for the people of Notting Hill bringing together racial
groups which otherwise might not have had much contact—and
the people in the area seem to be very pleased with what's happening.

21

Official hostility towards me extends far beyond the boundaries of Notting Hill. It involves interference with my telephone and my mail, obstruction by the United States Embassy and a visit from the Central Intelligence Agency.

The first time a member of my organisation phoned me and the phone didn't ring in my house even though he heard it sounding normally, I made a mild complaint to the General Post Office. Now I have to complain twice a week. People are always phoning me and the tone sounds perfect to them, so when they get no answer they assume I'm out. I can be sitting beside the phone waiting for their call, but it doesn't ring. When I lift the receiver, everything is perfectly normal so I'm unaware that anything's gone wrong until it's too late. It's a method of disrupting my communications, making life tough for a man who's trying to do something for his people. The GPO send a man round, all right. Sometimes he says it was a fault in the cable under the road and it's now been repaired; at others he opens up the instrument with a screwdriver and then screws it up again, telling me: 'It's all right now.' I've spoken to a great many people about this, but I can't find anyone else who has the same trouble.

It's a similar hang-up with the mail. Some of it never arrives at all. And sometimes, at my office, I'll get a whole heap of letters to do with the organisation all arriving the same day with anything up to ten days difference between the postmarks. Some of these letters are urgent and their non-arrival can be terribly destructive. People just assume you aren't answering your mail, are not interested, etcetera. Destroy a man's communications and you stand a good chance of destroying the man.

The first trouble I had with the American Embassy was soon after Malcolm died. I made a rather late decision to attend his funeral and, after checking plane times, provisionally booked a day ahead on an evening flight which would get me to Chicago in time. I went to the embassy the morning before and told them I wanted a visa to attend a funeral. At first they told me I couldn't have one, but when I pursued the matter and insisted on knowing why not, they said they would let me have one as long as I provided proof that I had funds to keep me while I was in America and could show I was a responsible person who was returning to Britain.

I raced around and got everything they wanted : letter from the bank, marriage certificate, children's birth certificates. It took the remainder of that day, but I went to the embassy next morning to collect the visa. Then they sprang on me the fact that my return ticket was not sufficient proof that I was returning; I must get a lawyer's letter to confirm it.

I managed to get this letter by midday and then I was told the official handling my case was not available. I said I had to catch a plane at 6 p.m., but they were adamant that nobody could deal with it but this one guy. I waited. He came back about 4.30 p.m. and it turned out he had a lot of people to see before me and that's the way it had to be. I finally got my visa at 7.30 p.m. after the embassy had closed. They let me out of the back door—too late to get to the funeral, with merely the hollow triumph of having got the visa out of them.

Some months later I wanted again to make a trip to the United States, to spend a few days with the Honourable Elijah Mohammed, with whom I'd been corresponding. This time at the embassy they refused outright to give me a visa.

'But I had one,' I said, 'and it's run out. I simply want to renew it.'

This fellow across the desk, who came on as if he were the biggest man in the American Administration, told me : 'I'm afraid we made a mistake last time. That visa should never have been issued.'

'Why not ?' I demanded. 'What have I done ?'

I had, he told me blandly, contravened section two-hundred-and-something of the Act.

'What the hell does that mean?' I said.

'I'm afraid I'm unable to answer that question,' he said.

'Do you have any literature about this Act that I can study?' I asked.

He handed me a form which listed all manner of offences which would prevent the granting of a visa. They ranged from drug peddling to sexual crimes against minors. I had never been accused, let alone convicted of any of these things.

'What has this to do with me?' I asked. 'Which of these crimes am I supposed to have committed?'

'I am not at liberty to say,' he replied. 'Perhaps you would like to tell me what you have done.'

It was a complete comic scene, but at the time I didn't see the funny side of it. In fact, I blew my cool. I demanded to see his superiors and when he told me loftily that he had none, I gave him a rousing speech on how easy it was for anyone to get into the United States. I had sailed the Great Lakes quite a bit as a seaman and I was aware of scores of places both there and in the South where one could cross the border with impunity.

'This is quite stupid,' I told him. 'You are forcing me to show up the weakness of your own security system. Anyone can get into the United States.'

He stared at me blankly. There was nothing more I could do.

It was only a few days later that a West Indian friend of mine rang me. He was a writer who did a lot of work for newspapers and knew all kinds of people. He told me a man had arrived in London who wanted to see me; it was important that I should meet him because he was in the Central Intelligence Agency. I said that was perfectly all right and stated a time for him to come.

The bell rang on the dot and I opened the door to this big, handsome, rather swarthy man in a beautifully cut dark light-weight suit. He looked me straight in the eyes and said: 'I am the person you're expecting.'

I invited him in and introduced him to Nancy. 'My name is Roy Wilson,' he said. 'Nice place you have here.'

I offered him a drink or coffee, both of which he declined, and I asked him if he liked records and put something on the record player. He glanced around the room while we listened to the music and then he put his hand in his pocket and said: 'I've brought you a present.'

He handed me a photograph, a picture of Malcolm X.

'It was taken just a couple of minutes before he was shot,' he said. 'I thought you'd like it.'

'Thanks very much,' I said. 'It's a beautiful picture.'

Nancy went to another room at this point in order to leave us alone and Roy Wilson tapped the camera hung around his neck with a well manicured hand and asked in a polite, educated voice : 'May I take a few pictures while I'm here.'

'Go ahead,' I said. People are always taking pictures of me and I figured, why say no—I might as well let them have decent ones.

From then on he started snapping all the time. He took quite a few shots of me and when I moved to the record player I would hear him clicking like mad.

'I love pictures,' he said.

He was certainly a keen photographer. He must have snapped the whole room.

At one point I put on an Aretha Franklin record and he said : 'Malcolm was very fond of her too.' Which was true and revealed that he really knew Malcolm.

We had a certain amount of small talk about the records and I told him there was a very good ice cream parlour nearby and I would go and fetch us some ice cream if he cared for some. England, I explained, made terrible ice cream generally, but this particular parlour was as near to American standard as you would find. He said he did like ice cream and maybe we could visit it a little later. He added that Malcolm had been very fond of ice cream parlours.

We began to talk about England and the racial scene here and he asked me : 'How active are the brothers? How are things over here?'

By the 'brothers' he meant the members of RAAS. 'Peace and love, brother,' is our greeting.

'We're pretty new,' I told him, 'and we have quite a lot of things to do, but things are moving—slowly, but moving.'

He nodded and I went on to tell him how I'd been going to the United States to have a look at the scene there, but the American Embassy had refused me a visa. I said I couldn't understand their attitude.

'What are you going to do about it?' he asked.

I said I didn't know right then, but that America was a very easy country to get into if one had a strong reason for going and I couldn't believe the American Government didn't know that.

He nodded and said he'd just come from America and some of the black organisations there had very good programmes. CORE and SNCC, particularly, he said, had very good educational programmes for people in the South. They were doing a very worthwhile job.

He was charming and courteous and his tone didn't change as he went on : 'But true power they have not got. Let me tell you what power really means. . . . If you walked into the street, for example, and someone shot and killed you, they would be arrested, tried by the law of the land, convicted of murder and suffer the penalty. . . . But if I were to shoot you, I would simply show my badge and there would be no comeback. I have a licence.'

We sat in silence for a moment while I considered this strange statement and then I said : 'I have my work to do and I'll do it regardless of what might happen. If something sad like that came to pass I'd just have to accept it as part of my job.'

He smiled then and stood up.

'Do you think we could have that ice cream now ?' he said.

'Sure,' I said.

At the ice cream parlour I had a banana split and he had two scoops of chocolate and vanilla with hot chocolate sauce. We chatted a little about ice cream parlours elsewhere and then he bade me a courteous goodbye and left. I never saw him again.

22

My expanding activities have not only brought about hang-ups, however. Apart from constructive work there has been quite a bit of fun and a landmark in this was the poetry festival held in Cardiff in September 1965 as part of the Commonwealth Arts Festival. I'm sure the organisers would like to forget it, though I'm sure they never will.

I'd first heard about it at Alex Trocchi's house. He knew one of the organisers and had been invited to represent Scotland. He asked me if I would be willing to represent Trinidad and read some of my poems at the festival. I said I would and expected to hear no more about it.

But with this particular festival, the system was for poets and writers to put forward the names of others they felt should represent their respective countries, and Alex and a number of beat poets I'd met through him put my name forward.

When I duly received my invitation, I had very mixed feelings about it. My own poetry had improved through discussions and readings at Alex's place, but Trinidad has some fine poets who relate the life and problems of the country through song. The greatest of them is a man called 'The Mighty Sparrow' and there was no doubt in my mind that he should be representing his country in my place. But although he's known throughout the West Indies, 'The Mighty Sparrow' has only limited appeal beyond those islands and as my poetry dealt with England and had been published here, I suppose I was better known in this country than he was. I accepted the invitation on the understanding that I could put over some of his work about the West Indies as well as my own.

It was a long time since I'd been to Cardiff and the circumstances of my present visit were very different from those of the former days. I had always lived in the dockland slums of Tiger Bay during my life as a seaman, but now I found myself booked into one of the best hotels in the elegant white city. I was one of some seventy poets arriving from all over the world to take part in the festival and a large section of the hotel with all its facilities had been—terribly rashly—placed at our disposal by the organisers.

The whole of Cardiff was excited about the festival and the hotel was already in a state of confusion when I arrived. Seventy poets gathered together anywhere are not exactly conducive to perfect order, and they had masses of fans and followers sprawling all around the beautiful lounges and milling about in the foyer. The management had not yet decided which rooms were for which poets, and the visitors were happily killing time ordering tea and biscuits and free drinks at the bars for themselves and their guests.

I was surrounded by newspapermen calling me Michael X and wanting to know if I was going to start a branch of RAAS in Cardiff. I thought it politic to escape and visit my old friends in Tiger Bay while the hotel chaos got sorted out.

I was very happy to see the Bay again. I met a lot of people I had known who were glad to talk to me as I'd always been thought of as something of a home town boy. But I was disappointed with the appearance of the Bay. Gone were the dilapidated old terraced houses which had given it a quality of tattered elegance and in their place were massive blocks of council flats. Although comparatively new, they were showing the results of bad workmanship with peeling paint and cracking plaster. The whole area had become a dismal slum and I felt very sad for my black friends.

The next morning the hotel was a colourful sight, with poets of all nationalities gathering in their little groups and making their way to the huge conference hall nearby. We sat in the terraced, semi-circular theatre for the whole morning, listening to the mayor and sundry officials going through the dreary procedure of long welcoming and explanatory speeches. In the afternoon we heard a few poems from the Welsh and Canadian representatives and it was all very proper and sedate.

But in my own mind I was working feverishly on a poem about the current conflict between India and Pakistan over the Rann of Kutch, with China breathing ominously down their necks, and I finally suggested at one of the mealtimes that the festival was a good occasion for us to try to do something positive about this conflict. The group I was with agreed, though we couldn't immediately think of the best action to take.

The idea continued to take shape in my mind and that night I suggested the poets should send a collective message to Mao Tse-tung asking him not to get involved in the war, not to risk its escalation. This produced a schism in the poets around me. Those for the idea included a number from Africa and India together with Alex Trocchi and the British beat poets. Dead set against it were a number of West Indians, who, with their middle class mentalities, didn't want to have anything to do with the likes of me and my subversive ideas.

I began to lobby in the hotel lounges, arguing the case and seeing how many poets I could count on to support a motion that we send a message to Mao. Before I went to bed I had more than half the conference behind me.

The following day the poetry reading continued and when it came to my turn I mounted the platform and confronted a theatre so packed it was bursting at the seams. Word had got around about what was going to happen and, apart from the poets, there were scores of students and dozens of press men filling the hall.

I began by saying I reckoned I rated a poor second to a fine poet like the Mighty Sparrow, who should really be representing Trinidad in my place, but that what I had to say was nothing directly to do with Trinidad. It had to do with a dangerous situation that was currently developing in the world.

There had been a little talking amongst the overflow of the audience in the wings outside the hall, but now it stopped and there was a deathly hush.

'I would like to raise a motion that this conference send a message to Chairman Mao Tse-tung, whom we consider a fellow poet, asking him to use poems against India—if he must use any-thing—and not guns,' I said.

A press man staring at me from the foot of the platform stood up and held his microphone out towards me.

'Mr Michael X from Trinidad, would you please repeat your motion so that we can be sure to get it on tape,' he said.

I repeated it slowly and immediately the poet Daniel Richter leapt to his feet and begged to second the motion.

Pandemonium then broke out.

The journalists began writing like mad; everyone else started talking at once. The Guyana delegate sprang to his feet and shouted that it was rubbish, that he strongly objected to the conference being used for political motives. Others yelled him down and a chorus of voices began calling for the vote.

At this point the festival director, Mr Bill Harpe, stood up on the platform looking a little bemused. He called for order and said he hadn't expected to see the conference taking this turn, but if that was the way it was going—with a shrug—so let it be.

While he was speaking, the chorus swelled up again : 'Vote, vote, vote, vote,' punctuated with cries of 'yes' and 'no'.

Bill Harpe asked for more discussion on the motion before a vote was taken, and ideas began to flow around the hall : that we should write a poem to Mao; that we should *all* write poems to Mao; that *I* should write a poem to Mao; that I should write a poem to Mao and submit it to the conference. . . .

The discussion went on for about an hour before it was settled that all who wanted to write poems should do so and that I should arrange for them to be sent to Mao. The motion was then carried with the support of more than seventy-five per cent of the conference.

Altogether twelve poets brought me their poems that evening for dispatch to the Chinese leader. They were all so good, but there was one I liked more than any of the others. In fact, I wanted to send just that one as an expression of the feeling of the poets' conference, but I was overruled. It was written by an Indian named Reginald Massey. I didn't know him and I've never seen or heard of him since, though his beautiful poem is with me constantly. This is it :

NIGHTMARE
(To Mao Tse-tung, poet)

Last night
That black cloud
Mushroomed
consumed.

> Himavant*
> sank back to the sea
> Tsang-po irrigated the desert†
> with blood.
> The flowers in your garden,
> had withered.
> But a solitary star
> pierced the curtain,
> Awoke me
> pitilessly.
> I did-not curse
> No I did-not curse.

The dispatch of the poems was taken over for me by the Cardiff evening newspaper, the *South Wales Echo*, whose editor offered to send them on at a party he'd given for the poets. I understand they were passed on to Reuters, who were prepared to send them only if the lines were run together. Since we'd stipulated they must in no way be mutilated, that wouldn't do. Finally the New China News Agency sent them in their poetic form at some expense.

Some six weeks later a telex message arrived at my house. It was from Mao, thanking me for the beautiful poems. He never did interfere in the Indo-Pakistani dispute.

From the second day on the chaos and confusion at the hotel increased. The poets took over the building. When they were not reading their poems at the lecture theatre, they were holding sessions, surrounded by devoted fans, in every nook and cranny of their new pad. You'd find the junkies in their rooms turning on, the drinkers swilling back the liquor, the hungry ones eating enormous meals and inviting their fans to partake of all the good things offered on the menu. Some of the more cosmopolitan types began telephoning their friends in Hong Kong, Adelaide, New York, all over the world, inviting them to the scene. All of the young girls in Cardiff and beyond seemed to be making themselves available and were all over the poets' rooms—and the poets—all hours of the day and night.

The regular guests inevitably began complaining about the 'goings on' and an employee of the hotel confronted us one even-

* Himavant means, I am told, the Himalayas.
† Tsang-po is a river in China.

184 FROM MICHAEL DE FREITAS

ing and told us that the ladies really must be out of the hotel at
night.

At that, Alex Trocchi rose up from amidst his admirers at the
far end of the lounge, like a genie from a lamp, and sternly
retorted : 'What do you expect? Throughout history poets have
been great lovers. It's perfectly right and natural that all these
ladies should be here with us.' He went on in a resonant speech
to imply that anyone who disagreed was impotent.

Thereafter outgoing telephone calls began to be vetted and
special meal cards were issued to prevent unauthorised persons
from eating free. Even this brought retaliation from a group of
poets who collected all the shoes left outside the doors one night,
hid some and mixed the others up. In the morning, the hotel was
full of attractive girls who shouldn't have been there at all running around with men's shoes in their hands, and distinguished
gentlemen of various nationalities, who wouldn't normally be
seen with a tiepin out of place, roaming distractedly around in
their bare feet. As the chambermaids hunted high and low for
the missing footwear, one could hear them saying : 'Never known
anything like this' . . . and 'I'll be glad when it's all over.'

I don't think the hotel had realised what they were letting
themselves in for. They'd figured a poets' conference wouldn't
be that different from a miners' conference.

By the fourth day, things were really hotting up. Poets who
had nothing to do with the festival started arriving at the hotel
with the festival followers—girls who follow the poets around
like camp followers follow the soldiers. I remember one American
poet-follower who'd come down from the Edinburgh Festival.
She was nineteen and looked fourteen, with mousey hair and
spectacles and a certain amount of grime hiding an attractive
face and body. She wore a sheepskin coat and purple stockings
with holes in them. She came from Chicago and looked as if she'd
hitch-hiked non-stop across the Atlantic. She didn't write herself;
she just loved poets and writers. She went through those poets
like collecting their autographs, passing from one to another,
since she had nowhere to stay, and just loved them all.

When it began to get really wild with train loads of beatniks
coming in answer to the phone calls, I figured it would be wise to
leave. The night before I moved out, I told one of the young
poets that I was going back to London because I had a lot of
work to do and I asked him when he was thinking of leaving.

'When it's over,' he said. This particular poet had spent the summer living in some famous beatnik caves under the cliffs near Cassis in the South of France. Before that he'd been in Tangiers. He probably hadn't had a square meal for a year or two before Cardiff. He began to recount to me his food consumption that day. He'd ignored the early morning tea on account of the fact that he'd been too hungover from the free alcohol of the night before, but with a great effort he'd made the breakfast schedule and faced the day with orange juice, porridge, eggs and bacon, toast, tea and bread and jam; he'd been in the lounge for coffee and biscuits at eleven and for lunch he'd waded through brown Windsor soup, roast beef, roast potatoes, Brussels sprouts and Yorkshire pudding, mixed fruit salad and cream, Cheddar and Caerphilly cheese with biscuits followed by coffee; 3.30 p.m. had found him back in the lounge for watercress sandwiches, toasted scones, cakes with pink icing and his individual pot of tea with lemon; at dinner he'd sat down to minestrone soup, steak and kidney, mushroom and oyster pie with French beans and boiled new potatoes, ice cream, Wensleydale and Double Gloucester cheese and more coffee; from then on until alcohol had overcome him once more he'd tucked into late night cheese and tomato, ham and egg, and lettuce and shrimp sandwiches.

'I've never eaten so well in my life,' he concluded. 'I've put on six pounds ready for the winter. I'm not leaving until I have to.'

I moved out on the fifth day of the festival, just in time to keep my sanity. The conference had spilled out of the hotel so that the whole of Cardiff seemed to be embroiled. Groups of poets were meeting in parks, making plans for happenings. Someone was working on bringing in Mick Jagger. The beatniks continued to arrive in ragged groups to be greeted like desert travellers by those already at the oasis of the hotel.

One American poet who had been impressed with the success of my Mao motion wanted to raise another against the war in Vietnam. He proposed to show the conference what Vietnamese blood looked like in order to dramatise the issue. He was planning to steal a Vietnamese pig from Cardiff Zoo and slaughter it with a bow and arrow on the stage of the lecture theatre. Another American, Doc Humes, had decided to write an action novel. Somehow everyone was to have a part in it. . . .

It was anarchy.

I don't know how much longer the conference went on. I do know it was the first major poetry conference to be held in Wales and will probably be the last. And that Mr Gulbenkian, whose Foundation sponsored the whole thing, paid the final, ghastly bill.

I still have a copy of the message Prince Philip sent the festival from Buckingham Palace, emphasising the importance of appreciating the diversity of the cultural background of the Commonwealth: 'This festival will bring together a wide variety of groups and art forms as a living and exciting demonstration of the scope of human imagination within the Commonwealth,' he said. 'I hope the occasion will encourage visiting artists . . . to meet and indulge in stimulating shop talk. It could well prove a landmark in the development of the arts. . . .'

It was certainly all of that.

23

For me, one of the most interesting aspects of the Commonwealth Arts Festival was that I was able to meet a large number of West Indian artists and creative people. We had quite a lot of discussion about racial problems and organisation and I found that although their aspirations were often very middle class, they had a much greater sympathy for the plight of the downtrodden black man and what we were trying to do for him than did the black, intellectual bourgeois. These artists, poets, dancers, musicians saw the ghetto man as a person, whereas the black bourgeois—the doctors and lawyers—are not willing to see him as a human being at all. It's impossible to discuss him with them; we don't speak the same language.

The creative people could really groove with the ghetto man and understand the pain and torture he went through. So I would tell them stories of the ghetto—which was the ground for much of my recruitment for RAAS.

I would tell them about the gas meter robber, whose mentality is difficult to understand. He will go into a house in the area where he lives and break open a gas meter belonging to his friend, neither understanding nor caring that it's his friend who gets the bill for the damage, that it's his friend he's actually robbing. If his friend were to surprise him in the middle of the operation, the meter robber would actually pull out a knife and cut him up to escape—all over a few, measly shillings.

I would tell them about the hustlers sitting in the gaming houses, broke. How a white prostitute would knock on the door, peek in and ask : 'Is Joe here?' and one of the hustlers would very sharply say : 'No, he's just gone down the street, but he said to leave it for him,' and how the woman would give him her takings for the evening saying : 'Tell him I've gone home.' There is no honour among these thieves.

I would tell them what I knew of the hopelessness of hustling. There was the example of Big Jim, a very handsome Trinidadian in his thirties who was living high when I first came to England. I used to look up to him then. He talked to any and everybody in a loud, confident voice, and he always had a red carnation in his buttonhole. He had come during the war after a spell of working on ships and when he arrived in Britain he had the same problem I had—he just couldn't get a job and decided to give up trying. Big Jim had one woman hustling for him in the East End who gave him £200 a week—I know this because sometimes he sent me to collect his wages—and he had other women working for him too. I saw him a few months ago, dead broke, fighting over a half-crown.

The hustler lives an empty life in a miserable tenement and he must make flamboyant gestures. In a dark gaming house I've seen someone drop a shilling and light a five pound note with a match to look for it. That act is typical of the hustler's compulsive ostentation. In the Grove, you'll find him driving a big car with a big, beautiful blonde chick at his side and it looks as if things are really happening with him. But it's all façade. The car's not paid for, the woman's not staying and although he's making money, his mind's deteriorating faster than he can spend the bread. The hustler has no idea what's happening in the world, with his people, anything. He knows nothing of life except the price of a gross of French letters or a gaff for his woman to hustle in. When the woman leaves him for another hustler, he's completely lost and moons around waiting for another woman. His life is the shebeen, the gaming house and the woman as a commodity. It doesn't occur to him that he's selling his body and tomorrow that body will not have the same commercial value it did yesterday. He thinks the woman is the only one selling. If, by some misfortune, he gets his woman pregnant and she grows too big to hustle, there's a hell of a mess since he has no way to make money to look after the woman and the child. It's not unusual to see children running around in the streets of the ghetto picking up used French letters in dark alleys and blowing them up as balloons. The hustler doesn't look at what's happening.

The composition of RAAS is pretty varied : schoolteachers, bus conductors, nurses, students. . . . But I work hardest in the ghetto because that's where the need is greatest. I go into the gaming houses to see the hustlers since it's not possible to call them to a meeting. I might meet a hustler who's just lost his money gambling and he'll say : 'Michael, buy me something to eat,' and I will and I'll tell him he wouldn't be in that position if he banked his money. He's already on the defensive because he's lost his money and next time I see him I'll take him with whatever he has in his pockets to a bank and open an account for him and take away his bank book. This is a necessary first step to giving him a bit of solidity and moving him out of his ambience altogether. He'll let me do this because he thinks I'm very rich and successful and have a powerful organisation going. If I were walking around hustling for pennies he wouldn't listen.

The next thing that happens is he comes to my house and I cook for him and for other hustlers who are also visiting and we sit around and talk about life and being black and the problems of living and what can be done about it. And it's a big scene for the young hustler, just to be out of the ghetto, seeing something else, talking and hearing talk about something beyond his immediate needs. Before he goes, he says : 'Can I come again?' and he does and finally he ends up working for RAAS and when he goes back to the ghetto he doesn't go near the shebeen; he distributes leaflets instead.

I have to win the hustlers one at a time. It's not an easy job. If you make an approach in the wrong place or use the wrong methods, you are told to fuck off. That's why it helps to know the scene. They all know that I am them, too.

Some time back we held an illegal blues dance in a basement in Reading. It was organised by some of my non-Moslem field workers as I have had nothing to do with alcohol since I became a Moslem, but I did visit to see how things were going and I made a short speech into a microphone. I told them : 'I have come to rob you. You all know that. You know you're paying 2s 6d here for a beer that costs 1s 1d in a store. But what we're going to do with this money we've taken from you is to start a black barber's shop in this town where you can go and get your hair done properly and maybe after that we'll have some more

dances and go on robbing you and finally you'll have black restaurants here, too, where you can eat the sort of food you like
and that you can't get anywhere else.' Reading is a town with a
big black population and not a single facility for them and everyone applauded my words. They understood what I was saying and
they accepted my methods. They have their barber's shop now.

These methods, I know, are unorthodox. But you can't organise
the ghetto through a smart secretary and a tidy office. Lots of
organisations have talked about it, but no other organisation,
black or white, can do it. Only ghetto people can organise in the
ghetto.

The West Indian artists listened very sympathetically to my
stories and we established a certain rapport. But as soon as I
suggested they might come to the ghetto to give some joy to the
people living there, the middle class aspect of their personalities
came to the fore. Their first reaction was how much money could
they get and then their abhorrence for the ghetto began to come
out—the dirt, the violence. They wouldn't want to go inside the
ghetto at all.

I have introduced a number of American artists and personalities into the ghetto. People like Dick Gregory, Oscar Brown
junior and Mohammed Ali, the world heavyweight boxing champion, are happy to go there and talk to the people and entertain
them in any way they can for no financial reward whatsoever.
The West Indian artist will say that they have more money than
he does and can afford to do it. But that's not it at all. The West
Indian artist is quite well off—better off than I am, for instance,
and I'm still prepared to give myself to the ghetto. What's really
wrong is that the West Indian artist has had some of the West
Indian middle-class attitude rubbed off on him. It's a lack of
generosity between human beings. The West Indian middle class
are the most ungenerous people in the world. The British middle
class will send off a few shillings to Oxfam to ease their conscience; the West Indians won't even do that.

Dick Gregory, Oscar Brown junior, Mohammed Ali and others
like them really care about people and what's happening to them.
Dick and Oscar have sat in gaming houses I've taken them to and
wanted to know the thoughts of the people inside. They will ask
questions, sign autographs, entertain, put themselves at the disposal of the ghetto. They want to know their own people. That's
the difference. They care.

24

I first met Herbert Muhammed and Mohammed Ali, the incomparable world heavyweight boxing champion, while I was trying to make RAAS into a viable organisation. There had been quite a bit of correspondence with the Honourable Elijah Muhammed about what I was trying to do and what he had already done, and when it was decided that Mohammed Ali was going to Sweden to box exhibitions, the Honourable Elijah suggested I meet him and Herbert.

I will go anywhere to see anyone I want to talk to and I flew over to Stockholm and met them in the foyer of their hotel in the evening. We exchanged greetings and went up to Mohammed's room to talk.

I was very impressed with both of them in their different ways. Mohammed was a very beautiful boy and quite different from his publicity build-up. He was quiet and attentive and would sit in silence for hours listening while Herbert and I talked. He devoured every word Herbert said and clearly had enormous respect for him. I didn't find this difficult to understand because Herbert is very, very bright. His mind clicks over like mad. And he's straight, too, in the things he says. There's no question of hedging on anything.

Herbert and I sat and talked for three days, while Mohammed listened. Mostly we talked about organisation, but we also touched on Malcolm X because in the States I was very much identified with him. Herbert told me about the silencing of Malcolm by his father and the eventual split between them. He suddenly said: 'My father loved him like his own son. He would give him anything he wanted—anything. He loved him.' I felt there was something very deep behind these words and for a very brief moment it seemed to me that Herbert might have been jealous of his father's love for Malcolm.

He was critical of him, saying Malcolm could not bear to keep quiet and would not accept discipline. This did not ring true because although I knew Malcolm loved the limelight, he was a very hard disciplinarian—to himself as much as to others. It seemed to me it was painful for Herbert to discuss Malcolm and we never referred to him after that except for the odd occasion when Herbert said to me about something I was doing: 'You're just like Malcolm.'

Although Mohammed recognised it was principally Herbert I was there to see, he, too, would talk occasionally in his astonishingly articulate way. He was training at the time to be a Minister for the Nation of Islam and was already a pretty powerful speaker. He would tell me about the racial situation in America and clearly felt as strongly about it and as deeply involved as anyone could.

After this initial meeting, the correspondence between the Nation of Islam and RAAS increased, and at the time of the Ali-Cooper fight in London, the Honourable Elijah wrote and asked me if I would help look after Mohammed and Herbert while they were here.

They arrived some time before the fight: Mohammed, Herbert, Jimmy Ellis, Angelo Dundee, the whole entourage . . . there was even a photographer from *Mr Muhammed Speaks*. Herbert and Mohammed were the only Muslims in the group and since they were very eager to see what was happening on the racial scene over here, I had the opportunity to get to know them a whole lot better.

They attended a number of meetings that I addressed and though they sat inconspicuously in the body of the hall, the word had always managed to get around that the 'Champ' was present —and my audiences were more than double the usual number. There would be as many as six hundred people milling around— the extra number totally lacking the discipline of my own people and giving the stewards a hard time as they bobbed about trying to get a glimpse of Mohammed. He, in contrast, would sit in rapt attention in one of the front rows, apparently quite fascinated by my speeches. They were usually on rather different lines from those of his own Ministers in the States. Their themes would normally be religious with a trace of economics; mine would be social, economic and political.

It is a habit of mine to look at one particular face in the audience while I'm talking and Mohammed was such a very good listener and had such a nice face to look at that I generally ended up addressing myself to him.

His self-effacing interest in what was going on is typical of the man's more private life. He is a terribly nice, modest person, wide-eyed to see and hear everything and full of questions to which he really wants answers. The loud mouth and the poems were always strictly for the public.

Sometimes I went driving with him and Herbert through the London ghettoes of Brixton and Notting Hill. Mohammed would look around at the poverty and hopelessness and ask over and over again : 'What can I do to help these poor people?' His own answer to his question was that he should give them some of the obvious thing that he had a lot of : money. But he didn't understand the difficulties of distribution and all the problems it would produce. I told him a better idea was that he should go and talk to them. That would bring some real joy into their lives. He was very enthusiastic about this idea and I made arrangements for him to meet the people, particularly the children, of the Notting Hill area.

Mohammed loves children. He can make direct contact with them and he's very happy when he's with them. During the evening we spent in the ghetto he must have chatted and played with something like seventy of them. There was no discrimination. I'd already explained to him that I didn't believe in segregation of children and that at the London Free School, white and black people worked voluntarily together for the good of the community. He didn't query it. He figured I knew best how things should be done in Britain and I rather think he was advised before he left the States that over here he'd find things a little different. Anyway white and black children met the champion and found him equally happy to see them. He would turn up in a room and sit on the floor with them, chat and joke with them and take pictures with them. The kids would jump all over him. Sometimes you couldn't see him for children.

Mohammed went into quite a few houses and an aura of

G

excitement hung over the whole area while he was there. He captivated everyone he met and the serious questions that arose in his mind, but that he was too polite to ask people, were unleashed on me later : how much do these people earn ? Can they live on it ? What sort of rents do they pay ? Where else does the money go ?

We'd arranged to have a photographer along and he snapped the champion all the way. There was a lot of happiness in the ghetto that night. For many ghetto people one of their proudest possessions is the picture on the wall of Mohammed Ali making friends with the children of the family.

In the evenings Mohammed would usually retire fairly early and I would take Herbert around town to show him what black people did in the evenings. One place he'd heard of and wanted to visit was a club which was owned by a Jamaican I knew, so we went there one night.

The club is a large basement. You go in through a murky side entrance surrounded by big, tough-looking black men and waiting minicar drivers. It's fairly dark inside with a big ball spinning from the ceiling and reflecting different coloured lights from its facets : dark red, dark blue and other dark colours. The bar is on one side of the cellar and a stand with the orchestra is on the other. The people sitting around the walls and at the tables, and dancing, are mostly black hustlers of both sexes, but there are a few white women and white teenage boys and a number of pretty coloured chicks who just like to dance.

We sat in chairs near the musicians, listening to the Jamaican blue beat and digging the scene. A lot of pretty, coloured girls had seen us with Mohammed while they were after his autograph at the hotel and they recognised Herbert as a big name in the Nation of Islam. They wanted to be nice to him and they came and sat and talked with us and finally one of them asked him to dance.

Dancing is frowned upon in the Nation of Islam, but Herbert had a flair for relating to people in order to carry out his work. Everybody was dancing at this point and it was clearly the best way to relate to the young people there. So Herbert, who had never danced in his life before, moved out onto the floor. The girl began to show him the moves and he picked them up very well, grinning all over his face and looking back over his shoulder to tell me in great surprise : 'Look man, I'm dancing. I'm really dancing.'

Those sweet girls made Herbert very happy. He was fascinated by their beautiful footwork, which he likened to Mohammed's footwork in the ring. He loves being with young people and I think it's a pity he can't dance in the States since it's a nice enjoyable thing to do.

Shortly before the fight took place, I was showing Mohammed some essays I'd written about the English scene, one of which ended with the words : 'I know there will be blood on the streets, white man. And it's my concern to see that the blood will not be that of my people.'

Mohammed read it and shook his head.

'You don't want to shed your blood,' he said. 'After the fight I'll give you something.'

After the fight he gave me his shorts spattered with Henry Cooper's blood. 'Here's the blood of an Englishman for you,' he said. A boxing fan has offered a lot of money for those shorts, but I treasure them to this day.

When Mohammed returned to London for the fiasco with Brian London, I arranged for him to talk to a few bodies like the Islamic Students Group and he enjoyed doing it. He talked very softly and persuasively on his particular subject—physical fitness and what it does for you. He brought in the Muslim philosophy of bathing and cleanliness to support his thesis that physical fitness helped to produce a mental awareness that could improve one's life. It went without saying that he really knew what he was talking about. He is a fitness fanatic. The students were very happy to listen to him and the fact that he was an authority on his subject probably didn't matter to them. I think they would have been spellbound whatever he talked about.

I spent quite a lot of time with him, driving him around, showing him the usual tourist sights—where the Queen lives, Westminster Abbey, Nelson's Column . . . I began to recognise some very boyish qualities in him. I remember one conversation we had about the way anything he said attracted world-wide attention. I recalled his statement that he had no quarrel with the Viet Cong and said it would undoubtedly go down in history. He was astonished at this, since his idea of a famous statement was Joe Louis's wartime comment that the West would win because God was on our side. With his eyes wide, he wanted to know if his own statement was as great. 'Do you really think I'll go down in history?' he asked and was thrilled when I said I was sure he would. Often, too, before a fight, he'd sit in his hotel room and play the pop records he'd brought with him, talk about them and sometimes sing them in his very nice voice (he once made the Hit Parade with *Stand by Me*) as if he had no more pressures than a teenager enjoying himself.

His boyishness came out again after he'd beaten Cooper. We had to fight our way out of the milling stadium and then a huge limousine with police outriders carried us back to the hotel. Mohammed sat back in the deep leather with his eyes alight, happy as a kid on a roller coaster.

Not that women saw him as a little boy. The man exudes sex as far as they're concerned. They love him. I provided one of my men to do his secretarial work while he was in England and this poor guy was inundated with scores of letters every day from women who wanted to marry Mohammed and offered him everything. Some were rather funny to read; others a little pathetic.

Lots of women wouldn't leave it at a letter. They'd elude the hotel staff, arrive at his door and burst in begging to be allowed to go to bed with him. 'Just once, just once,' they would plead as they were politely but firmly ejected. Some of these ladies—who were usually very attractive girls, both white and black, in their twenties—would try to be more subtle. They'd knock on the door and say they wanted to talk to him about some business project, like advertising something or opening their new hair-dressing salon. We would weaken and let them in for a cup of tea and once inside they'd start feverishly stripping off their clothes and begging to stay the night with the champion. Some of them, who didn't seem to be wearing very much, were stark naked quicker than you could do the Ali-shuffle and would even make some wild attempt to rape Mohammed before Herbert or I, or anyone else in the room could get them out.

It's something that Mohammed is accustomed to and he was always very polite and kind to his would-be seducers. But to me it was quite astonishing to see how even thirteen-year-old school-girls would try to make him, and how women would reach out to touch him and have their legs give way at the contact so that they had to sit down. I never really got used to the idea that every night several women would sit outside his door and refuse to go until they were ejected by the hotel staff.

They turned up at his Shepherd's Bush training camp, too.

I remember one rather lovely black woman somewhere in her late twenties who arrived every day with a baby in her arms and a toddler by her side. She would just sit and watch the champion work out with adoration in her eyes. I spoke to her once and asked her: 'How come you are here every day?' She looked back at me and said, 'How could I stay away?' From the training camp she would make her way to his hotel and sit in the foyer with her babies, hoping for him to pass. Once Mohammed went and took the baby out of her arms and held it up, smiling. The woman's eyes just hung on him, adoring, and I don't think she even knew the child had gone from her hands.

I began to suffer from some sort of reflected glory. Women began to ring me up to say they wanted instruction in Islam and then they'd turn up with their suitcases.

The most curious example was a fourteen-year-old schoolgirl who had seen me with the champion and wrote to ask me about Islam. I sent her some literature and she wrote back to say she wanted to came to the mosque. Perhaps she thought this was the equivalent of etchings. She rang me at home, then, and asked if she could come over to talk. Unsuspectingly I said she could and so this very nubile young lady arrived at my flat. She started by telling me how very dissatisfied she was at home and how badly she got on with her parents. I made a few sympathetic noises and tried to get her to talk about her school and studies. Suddenly she gave up all pretence and said: 'Can't I stay with you?' I found this terribly embarrassing and began to say it wasn't really possible, wishing Nancy were home, whereupon she stood up, unabashed by the fact that I had someone typing in the next room, and took off her dress, saying: 'I'm staying'. I had to call the typist chick and ask her to handle the problem for me.

I learnt then, from my own experience, that it was always wise to have a couple of people in any room Mohammed was occupying because you can't really tell what amazing lengths women will go to. He even has his brother Rahman Ali, or Herbert, in the bedroom when he's asleep nowadays.

However, I don't think he loses any sleep over this popularity. It certainly doesn't appear so from his performances in the ring. In my view he's the best heavyweight there ever was. And if you see him shatter the heavy, sixty pound bag in training you realise that contrary to what his critics say, he has a knockout punch that could drop anyone. I have never seen him let go at a man with the viciousness he unleashes on the bag. I think he knows just how strong he is and that if he does use that kind of power against an opponent he'll kill him. I am sure he could have knocked out any of his opponents, but you don't see him extending himself in the ring the way he does in training. Cooper was a terrible mess, remember, and Mohammed didn't want to hit him at all. He was running away and not touching him. The film shows that very clearly.

I'm quite sure that if it were possible to put Mohammed Ali in the ring with any of the champions at their peak—Tunney, Dempsey, Louis, Marciano—he'd make mincemeat of them.

25

Once the aims of RAAS were clearly drawn up, we were able to go ahead consolidating and developing, which we did in many ways.

Our speaking techniques improved a lot and the subject matter expanded, for example. In my own case, when I first began speechmaking the only thing I was able to talk about was unity (we kept the tapes of our earlier speeches so that we could learn from them and when I hear mine now, I recognise they were very poor), but with confidence growing from experience, I found that my own problems would give me new themes. I would begin to talk, for instance, about the relationship between black men and women. I read a lot about society and women's role in Africa, America and elsewhere in the world so that I would get a broad view, and then I began urging for greater understanding between the sexes, spurred on by my own recognition that I had not appreciated my wife's problems the way I felt I should. I had always held the typical West Indian view that certain areas were women's work and men didn't help in those spheres. Now I began to urge that the black woman be given more consideration as a human being.

I also made speeches in the ghetto areas, where I would draw on my own experience to talk about hustling and the world of make-believe it is. I would ram it home to the gas meter robbers that it was not the Gas Board who suffered but the small man who ended up having to pay the bill. I described him as their brother and I told them: 'You don't destroy your brother.'

Another aspect of our development was the creation of our first business. It was a small co-operative clothing firm in Notting Hill. We hired two adjacent basements, joined them by knocking a hole in the wall, installed a few machines and brought together some sixteen people, who had previously been working on their own, to operate as a team. They had their separate jobs, sewing, selling and buying. The colourful dresses and hand-made shirts they produced for West Indians in the area sold very well and we brought in a couple of tailors to make suits as well.

Everybody in the business began to make quite a good living—considerably more than they would have working alone—and once they realised how effective this sort of pooling of skills could be, they gave their energy and talent to the project with great enthusiasm. Some of us began to do a public relations job for the business outside the ghetto area and, particularly since they were producing good clothes more cheaply than elsewhere, the co-operative began to collect a lot more orders.

We discovered at this time that if something like this got any sort of racialistic label, whether it was Black Muslim, RAAS, or anything else, business suffered considerably. So we began to play down the organisation's part to such a point that we simply didn't mention it. We even employed a young white woman to sell our products to white people. I must admit that the executive didn't completely approve of my insistence on realism in this respect, but they went along with it because it worked.

I was very pleased about the way the business was working because I saw it as one of the basic functions of the organisation. I was not so much interested in building a highly efficient industry, as determined to involve a lot of people in working together. It would not have been really constructive to have an automated industry. My idea was to develop a really big scene to cater for people all over the country, but, unfortunately, people skilled in the dress-making business turned out to be in short supply. The business is still going strong, though, and the number of workers has grown to about thirty. It was the first of many.

With development, we also began to increase our intelligence and broaden the knowledge of our young workers by having them travel for the organisation in other countries.

Patel and Jan Carew had, in fact, already left this country a little earlier—Patel for India with the double purpose of seeing his wife and reporting on the situation in his country with a view to establishing a branch of RAAS there; Carew to take a post with the *African Review* in Ghana.

These departures pushed me into railroading the travel plan. My feeling was that we needed to have a more detailed and personal knowledge of the black man's situation in the world as a whole, and since there was still a bit of money left from the Carmen interlude, I thought it could hardly be put to better use. So our representatives went off for periods varying from weeks to months to learn about what was happening in the United States, in Jamaica, the Middle East, Guyana, Trinidad. . . .

They would make contact with the appropriate embassies and high commissions in London, and with organisations in the country to be visited, and from there they would operate on the two levels of government and grass roots, absorbing all they possibly could about what was happening so that they could send back reports to this country. With the information, we were able to speak from the viewpoint of actual observation by our own people rather than guess about situations second-hand from the newspapers.

Our man in America, for example, was the guest of a variety of organisations, including the Nation of Islam, CORE, SNCC and other bodies whose leaders we had previously met when they came to London to see us after our early blaze of publicity. With them as his guides, he was able to cut through anything that was irrelevant and get straight to the heart of the racial situation in America and learn what was being done about it and where and how.

We had already learned something from our American counterparts. In my own case the benefit was rather unexpected and I gained it by observation rather than discussion.

My mentor was Martin Luther King whom I met at a party given by friends during a visit he made to London. The first time I met him, he walked over to me and gave me this terribly impressive handshake. He held my hand as if he really wanted to meet me, looked me in the eyes and said how pleased he was to meet me as if it came really from the heart. His handshake really meant something to me at that time because I had the most awful handshake in the world going—as if I didn't really want to meet anyone at all—and his approach made me question my own way of meeting people.

When I saw him again the next night at another party, he came up with the same brilliant handshake and was very pleased to meet me all over again. We had no conversation at all. I faded into the background and just watched him meeting people. If I wanted to talk about organisation, I did that with his team—who were all very impressive, too. But Martin Luther King I was simply quite happy to observe. What I learned from him was how a real professional works. Because that's what he is—a real professional. And by watching him I learned where I was lacking myself.

I think the most important thing we learned—or, rather confirmed—from our observation of organisations in America, particularly the Nation of Islam, was that you work much more effectively if you are not seen. We found that the assets to be gained from avoiding the limelight were far greater than the liabilities. All one did in hiring a church hall and talking to hundreds was to exercise one's oratorical skills. Much more constructive work could be done with small gatherings of from ten to fifteen people in some secluded environment.

Our work started shifting along these lines and this marked the beginning of our BLADES OF GRASS CAMPAIGN, which is our current mode of operation. The phrase came from a speech I made to supporters and field workers in London in which I told them to be as invisible and inscrutable as a blade of grass as they went about their work. Camouflage was the order of the day.

Adopting this approach, our field workers moved from town to town talking to non-members in cellars, coffee bars, private homes. Each roving field man created a field worker in the place he visited and this man in turn would gather small audiences ready for our next missionary.

On these 'invisible' tours, we no longer philosophised about the unity of the black man. Instead we became very practical, teaching how black people could pool resources to gain economic viability, working hard on overcoming their natural mistrust by showing how legal safeguards could be put up for the individual working in a team with several others. We found the results of this type of campaign were much better, much more solid than our barn-storming tours with the press spotlight on us. In Nottingham, to cite one example, our new members were able, in a matter of months, to open a restaurant, barbers' shops and other small businesses where previously nothing had existed at all.

We also discovered that people worked harder on a more subdued level. With large, publicised meetings there was great, short-lived enthusiasm. But in the new situation we were creating, with people living on the same street, meeting regularly for discussion groups and co-operating to make a living, much stronger bodies were established.

Outside pressures, too, strengthened our belief that underground methods were wisest. With the actions of the British Government revealing it as very racialistic—the new Immigration Law and Rhodesia—we realised we were operating in a very hostile society. One may talk about using guerrilla methods in such a society, but it's not easy where the territory is alien and you are outnumbered by fifty-three to one in a war which is cultural, economic and racialist.

Due to the fact that we were now working in the homes of the people, we began making much more contact with youth. This revealed a potentially explosive situation.

Many of the young black people in Britain were born in this country and have grown up knowing no other. At school—if there's no interference from parents—they get very friendly with white children of their own age. But when they leave school and start looking for a job for the first time they discover a serious colour bar. They go to the Labour Exchange with their equally qualified white friends and they find that the white boy gets a job and they don't. Their parents, being immigrants, are accustomed to this racialist scene and expect it, but the children don't, and won't accept it. When they find this colour bar directed at them they start building up a lot of resentment. They are natural candidates for an organisation like RAAS and they make much more energetic and serious workers than their parents ever would.

These groups of black youth, who find they can no longer mix with their white friends, provide a great field for someone like Jan Carew who believes in a strong physical wing to an organisation such as ours.

Jan, who has a black belt in judo, began forming little groups for young people interested in physical fitness—particularly judo and karate—some time back. Black people have always been talented at sport. You only have to consider the present crop of fine black boxers, runners, footballers, cricketers, basketball players. . . . He had no trouble at all in attracting a large body of enthusiastic youngsters.

His first gymnasium was a cheap converted basement with a

few mats in Finsbury Park. From this beginning other gyms and clubs sprang up in London and beyond. Black men who already had grounding in karate and judo came in to help when they saw what we were doing and, as our young men developed, so they would teach others at an inferior level. Jan Carew has now left this country to continue his writing elsewhere, but I am happy to say his work goes on.

When Mohammed Ali came to London for the Cooper fight, I thought it a good opportunity to reveal a little of what we were doing and provided a twenty-four-strong bodyguard for him. The guards were all big beautiful six-footers, superbly disciplined. They were polite, but very firm and efficient and they had not the slightest trouble clearing Mohammed's path in any crowd. They were very impressive. Even the press thought so.

I would like here to say that we are not out to overthrow anybody. That's not why black men run or box either. But nor are we prepared to turn the other cheek. The way things are developing now we don't have to.

For us, minority that we are, it's an essential thing to be strong. The so-called race riots of that hot summer in 1958 may have been something of a shower in a teacup, but the real race riots likely to explode in Britain within the next year or so will be a very different matter.

Black people in this country are much angrier than they were and they are also much more aware of their common identity. If I go into Notting Hill gaming houses these days, I find there are far more people sleeping inside them because they have nowhere else to go than ever there used to be. It's the same in the all-night cafés. There are always a few black men sleeping with their heads on the tables. They are tired and they can't find a place to live.

If I listen to these people in the gaming houses or the cafés, I find their conversation has one major theme : a huge resentment at their inability to find a house, a job, or other things they might want, simply because they are black. They are terribly angry that they have no money and very little chance of earning any. They are very much aware that things are getting worse for them and that they are not wanted by the vast majority of the British population. A lot of them come to me and tell me tales of hatred and rejection to which they've been subjected, and they end up saying : 'We've got to do something,' and more and more frequently they are adding : 'Remember the Jews in Germany . . . it could happen here . . . there are only a million of us. . . .'

The black man's distrust of the white man in this country, due to the white man's actions, has now reached a level where it may be irreversible. Sometimes I talk to West Indians who have white wives and regardless of what they might say to their wives in bed, they tell me : 'They are white first and we must always remember that. When the chips are down they are white, and they will think about that first—and we're not in that mob.'

This may sound ridiculous to some, but it's an instinctive feeling that's shared even by the intelligentsia of the black bourgeoisie. The final depth of distrust. They and their wives don't know each other.

As a result of this, I find I am very much against mixed marriages, not because I am against communication between black and white—I have no fear of losing my own identity—but because it is so very difficult for two people of such different cultures really to get across to each other.

As a corollary to this distrust, black people in Britain are becoming more and more aware of one another. Gone is the extreme West Indian individuality they brought with them. Now they are showing an increasing concern for their own race. Even black women sit discussing their situation together in the eating houses, which is something that never happened a few years back. And those who open their own businesses are very determined not to have white staff, which is a reaction to their not being allowed to work in white businesses.

The Immigration Law in this country is a very clear indication that blacks are an unwanted minority. The white liberal who walks around with wonderful views—and what a tiny minority of them would be anything but white if really pushed—says : 'That's the politicians. I am against all racial discrimination.' But that leads me to retort that he is responsible. 'Me?' he cries. 'How? Why?' And I tell him that his prime minister has done this with the leave of the politicians who are his elected representatives. 'But I can't do anything about them,' he says. And I tell him that if he didn't like them and what they were doing he would get rid of them. He's like the man in the street who professes not to be against blacks, that it's not his fault. How is it possible to live in a country and see a people oppressed and do nothing about it? The answer is that the present oppression represents the true feeling of the people as a whole. That's the kind of society we have in Britain today.

Look at the judiciary, the police, the armed forces.

Last year in Wolverhampton a hundred and fifty white savages attacked the house of a Jamaican family because they didn't like the colour of their skin. When six white people appeared before a magistrate the next day, he described the whole thing as a 'neighbourly dispute'! At the same time, no black man in this country is unaware of the bias of the police and what is one to think of the military when one considers what happened to coloured troops in Aden. Nobody can lightly dismiss the actions of these bodies and say, 'It's not us.' They represent power in these islands and ultimately power lies in the hands of the people. That's why I find it difficult to exempt from blame even a white man who shows some humanity to black men.

One also hears a lot of talk about 'compromise'. Some people tell me I should work with the black intelligentsia to get things changed. But the black intelligentsia are a tiny minority within a minority and so terrified of their own position, their own precarious foothold in this society, that they don't know the man from the ghetto and don't want to know him.

The mass of black people in Britain cannot compromise. They have no house, no job, nothing. Where and what do they compromise from? They can't sink any lower. The sad thing is that they've been driven into a situation from which anything at all is better. They have nothing to lose.

Within Britain, it's the English who have the outstanding role in oppression of the blacks. I find it very easy to talk to the Irish, or the Welsh, or the Scottish nationalists because they have this love of country and they respect me for loving my own. I love my country and will never be happy unless the ground I walk on there is mine (at present it's all owned by the English—the oil refineries, sugar estates . . . and all we have is a flag). But the Englishman does not have this love of country. He's of the opinion all the rest is his too. He still thinks in terms of Empire. Have you ever in your life come across an English nationalist? He doesn't exist. What makes the Englishman a difficult man to deal with is that he wants what's yours too and doesn't want you to have anything. Black people in this country are coming to a full realisation of this and now know where they stand.

This realisation is pushing things to flashpoint. Conditions in the ghettoes are intolerable and nobody's doing anything about them. The black people, who are not encouraged to live anywhere else, are paying more for their miserable accommodation there than whites are paying in other areas. And their resentment is growing.

When I speak at meetings in the ghetto, I can feel the new tension in the audience and when I take a hard line on television about the man living there, when I tell the nation in strong terms how he feels, I am saying just what he wants me to say for him.

The thoughts and voices in the ghetto are the same now as the thoughts and voices of our brothers in the United States. The black man walking through the slums of Notting Hill says: 'We should burn this fucking place down.' You hear it every day.

When the explosion does come it will be a very big one. And everyone will suffer.

Black and white.